# REVISE AQA GCSE (9-1)

# History
## CONFLICT AND TENSION IN ASIA, 1950-1975

# REVISION
## GUIDE AND WORKBOOK

Series Consultant: Harry Smith

Author: Rob Bircher

---

## Also available to support your revision:

Revise GCSE Study Skills Guide      9781447967071

The **Revise GCSE Study Skills Guide** is full of tried-and-trusted hints and tips for how to learn more effectively. It gives you techniques to help you achieve your best – throughout your GCSE studies and beyond!

Revise GCSE Revision Planner      9781447967828

The **Revise GCSE Revision Planner** helps you to plan and organise your time, step-by-step, throughout your GCSE revision. Use this book and wall chart to mastermind your revision.

> **For the full range of Pearson revision titles across KS2, KS3, GCSE, Functional Skills, AS/A Level and BTEC visit:**
> www.pearsonschools.co.uk/revise

# Contents

· · · · · · · · · · · · · · · · · · · · · · · · · · · · · · · ·

**A small bit of small print**

AQA publishes Sample Assessment Material and the Specification on its website. This is the official content and this book should be used in conjunction with it. The questions and revision tasks in this book have been written to help you revise the skills you may need for your assessment. Remember: the real exam questions may not look like this.

# Causes of the conflict

The Korean War (1950–1953) was a civil war (a war between citizens of the same country) that became an international conflict due to the developing Cold War between the USA and USSR.

See page 2 for more information on the Cold War.

USSR liberated northern Korea, USA liberated southern Korea

**Division** into North Korea and South Korea

Long history of foreign powers controlling Korea

The USA had supported the nationalists, not the communists, in the Chinese Civil War (1945–1949)

**Impact of the Second World War**

Strong **nationalism** and determination to create an independent Korea

US relations with China

**Causes of the Korean War (1950–1953)**

**Nationalism and civil war**

Communist China was suspicious that the USA planned to **invade** China

**Impact of the Cold War (1945–1991)**

**Conflict** because of different **ideologies**: **communism** and **capitalism**

The USA was worried about the **spread** of communism in Europe and in **Asia**

The USSR was growing stronger in the **Cold War**, for example it had its own nuclear weapons

Conflict led to **invasion** of South Korea by North Korea, triggering the war

This is an overview of the main causes of the Korean War. The following pages look at these in more detail.

**Containment** and the Truman Doctrine

International conflict in Korea

## Key terms

**Asia** – the world's largest continent, including the countries between the Ural Mountains in Russia and the Pacific Ocean.

**Conflict** – violence between groups, military forces, countries.

**Containment** – keeping something under control, stopping it spreading and becoming more powerful.

**Tension** – when people or countries do not trust each other and fear that conflict could soon occur.

**USSR** – The Union of Soviet Socialist Republics, also known as the Soviet Union. A communist union of 15 states, controlled by Russia.

## Key concepts

**Capitalism** – a system in which businesses are owned by private individuals (not the state), with the aim of making profit.

**Cold War** – a state of **tension** and **conflict**, stopping short of open warfare, between the USA and its allies (the West) and the USSR and its allies (the East).

**Communism** – a system in which the state controls production (for example, food, goods) and there is no private property, with the aim of equality.

**Ideology** – a system of ideas about how things should be run, how people should behave.

**Nationalism** – love for your own country, putting your country above everything else.

## Now try this

1 Look at the diagram on this page. Then cover it up and write down the four main causes of the Korean War.
2 Identify which of these four main causes led directly to the division of Korea into north and south.

# The Cold War

The USA and USSR were allies in the Second World War, but tension between them increased as the spread of Soviet control threatened the USA's interests first in Europe and then in Asia.

## The importance of the Cold War

The Cold War was a conflict between the two superpowers: capitalist USA and communist USSR. The Cold War contributed to the Korean War in two main ways:

1. Korea was divided into a communist North linked to the USSR and a capitalist South linked to the USA. Both sides wanted a united Korea, but neither side would accept the other's ideology.

2. The USA was very concerned about the spread of communism. The USA was prepared to help defend any country threatened by a communist takeover.

### The United Nations (UN)

The United Nations was set up to help countries work out tensions between them. The UN **Security Council** was made up of the USA, the USSR, China, Britain and France. The Security Council makes decisions about what the UN should do to help solve disputes between countries, which includes using military force. However, Cold War tensions between the USA, the USSR and China made this more difficult.

### The Truman Doctrine

The USSR broke its promises to allow free elections in countries that its army had freed from Nazi control in the Second World War. Instead, communist governments took over Eastern European countries with Soviet support, forming the 'Eastern bloc'.

The Truman Doctrine was the USA's policy (announced by President Truman) to try to contain communism. The USA would support free people to resist takeover by communist powers. As a capitalist country, the USA was opposed to communist ideology and wanted to encourage capitalism and free trade.

## Key events of the Cold War

### Timeline

**October 1945 United Nations** set up, representing 51 nations.

**June 1947** The US Marshall Plan provides aid to rebuild Europe. The USSR prevents **Eastern bloc** countries from accepting this aid.

**August 1949** The USSR successfully tests its own atomic bomb.

**June 1950** Korean War begins.

**July 1953** Korean War ends.

**August 1945** US **atomic bombs** dropped on Japan. Japan surrenders, the Second World War ends.

**March 1947** President Truman promises that the USA will help any country threatened by communism – the **Truman Doctrine**.

**April 1949 NATO** forms: an organisation of the USA and allies in which each country will act to defend another member if it is attacked.

**February 1950** Senator McCarthy stirs up an anti-communist 'Red Scare' in the USA.

**March 1953** USSR leader Stalin dies.

**December 1954** NATO agrees that it would have to use nuclear weapons against any Soviet attack.

Chinese communists carrying pictures of Stalin, the leader of the USSR. This photograph from 1951 was taken at celebrations for the anniversary of the communist victory in the Chinese Civil War.

### Now try this

Explain why President Truman thought communism should be contained. Give **one** reason.

# US relations with China and Korea

When China became a communist country, the USA became much more determined to prevent other Asian countries from becoming communist, too. This was important for the Korean War.

## US reactions to communist China

China was the most highly populated country in the world. It had great potential power.

- The USA gave millions of dollars in aid to the nationalists fighting the communists in China's civil war. The USA also provided most of their military equipment.

- When the nationalists lost, critics in the USA thought their government had 'lost' China to communism by not being tough enough. This made the government want to 'get tough' in the future.

- US government officials became convinced that the USSR was responsible for China becoming communist, as part of a plan to spread communism worldwide.

- Only the USSR acknowledged the new Chinese state in 1950 (Treaty of Friendship). Instead, the USA gave aid to Taiwan and called for the nationalists to represent China in the UN.

- In 1950, US senator McCarthy began a campaign against communists in the USA, whom he blamed for weakening the USA. Americans were scared that communists were working to take over the USA too.

## Nationalism in Korea

- Korea was ruled by Japan from 1910–1945. There was opposition to the hated Japanese rule and nationalism increased.

- The nationalists aimed to create an independent, free Korea. But peaceful demonstrations were crushed by Japanese troops, with thousands killed.

- Many Korean nationalists escaped to China. Some joined with Chinese communists to fight against the Japanese. One of these was Kim Il-Sung, a Korean communist who became a guerrilla leader.

- Other nationalists in China tried to set up a Korean government-in-exile, ready for when Korea was free from the Japanese.

- After the Second World War ended, the USA set up a military government in South Korea. The USA kept Japanese officials as administrators over Koreans, and banned a Korean nationalist government. Korean nationalists strongly resented this.

China, Japan's enemy, gave support to Korean nationalists. The nationalists all wanted to create an independent, strong Korea, but they did not agree about how this should be done.

Korea in 1950. For centuries, Korea had been controlled by China and Japan. Now the USA worried about a communist Korea controlled by China and the USSR. They feared its fall would encourage more Asian countries to turn to communism: the so-called 'Domino Theory'.

## Now try this

1 'By 1950, the USA thought it was losing the Cold War to communism.' Write **two** points that support this statement.
2 State **one** way in which China helped Korean nationalists.

You could refer back to page 2 to help you answer this question.

# The division of Korea

Korea was divided into two in 1945. The leaders of North and South Korea both wanted the country reunited, but the North wanted a communist Korea and the South a capitalist Korea.

## Why was Korea divided in 1945?

- The USSR had liberated North Korea from Japanese forces in August 1945. As Cold War tensions built, the USA worried about the USSR moving south into the area they had occupied, taking control of the whole of Korea for communism.

- This was why the USA suggested dividing Korea. They used the 38th parallel because it split the country roughly in half, keeping the capital city Seoul in the USA's half.

The Korean people were not consulted about the division.

- The USSR agreed, probably because the USA had stronger forces than the USSR in Korea, as well as access to atomic bombs.

- The plan was that the UN would soon oversee elections to reunite Korea and make it independent.

The 38th parallel is a line of latitude: a line across the Earth running parallel to the Equator. There were 16 million Koreans in the South and 9 million Koreans in the North.

## The leader in the North: Kim Il-Sung

Kim Il-Sung in 1949

Elections to reunite Korea never took place. In 1948, a communist called **Kim Il-Sung** took control of the North without elections.

- Kim Il-Sung was a Korean nationalist who had fought the Japanese.

- He was determined to lead an independent, united Korea.

- Kim had lived in the USSR and became a major in the USSR's Red Army.

- The USSR supported Kim because he would follow Stalin's orders.

- The USSR supplied North Korea's military with heavy weapons, including tanks.

- Kim's communist government took land away from rich landlords for poor peasants to use. Peasants liked this.

- In September 1948, the North became the **Democratic People's Republic of Korea**, with Kim Il-Sung as its leader.

- Kim repeatedly asked Stalin to back an invasion, launching raids into the South.

## The leader in the South: Syngman Rhee

Syngman Rhee in 1949

Elections did go ahead in South Korea in 1948. **The Republic of Korea** was created. **Syngman Rhee** was elected as its president.

- Syngman Rhee was a Korean nationalist, who had spent time in jail for protesting for independence.

- He was determined to lead an independent, united Korea.

- Rhee had lived in the USA, where he trained to be a lawyer.

- The USA supported Rhee because he was strongly opposed to communism.

- Rhee was worried about a communist takeover. His security forces arrested suspected communists and put them in jail. People were not allowed free speech in case this increased opposition.

- Rhee called on the USA to help overthrow the North, determined to root out communism in all of Korea.

- However, the USA did not supply the South Korean military with heavy weapons like tanks, in case they were used to invade the North.

## Now try this

Explain why the division of Korea helped cause the Korean War. Give **two** reasons in your answer.

# Invasion by the North

On 25 June 1950, troops from North Korea invaded South Korea. The reasons for the invasion were partly due to tensions within Korea, and partly to do with superpower tensions.

## Why was there no invasion before 1950?

Kim Il-Sung requested permission from the USSR to invade the South several times before 1950. But Stalin refused because the situation was too risky due to Cold War tensions:

| Pre-1950 | 1950 |
|---|---|
| US forces in South Korea: an invasion would pull the USA in, which the USSR did not want. | US forces withdraw: Soviet intelligence said the USA was focused on Japan. |
| The USSR had no atomic weapons until August 1949, making the USA much stronger. | The USSR now had its own bombs to defend against the USA. |
| China was fighting a civil war, so could not support the invasion. | The communist triumph in China's civil war means China can support the invasion. |

In 1950, Stalin agreed to support Kim Il-Sung's invasion plans.

## Support for the invasion from the USSR and China

Stalin would not send Soviet troops, in case this triggered war with the USA.

Stalin said that the invasion could only go ahead if China agreed to support it.

He continued to supply North Korea with weapons, including tanks, artillery and aircraft.

Soviet generals went to North Korea to help Kim plan the invasion.

Because the USA had not used its military power to stop communism in China, Stalin thought they would not use it to defend South Korea.

This propaganda poster, called 'Long live indestructible friendship and cooperation', showing Stalin greeting Mao, is from 1950. Mao was the leader of the Chinese Communist Party, ruling China.

North Korea had sent thousands of fighters to support the communists in China's civil war.

China sent around 70 000 Korean fighters back to North Korea, along with weapons.

China promised to support North Korea's invasion with reinforcements if needed.

China moved large numbers of its own troops closer to the border with North Korea.

China was worried that the USA might still attack to return China to the nationalists.

## Events of the invasion

| 25 June 1950: troops from North Korea attacked all along the 38th parallel. | South Korean forces had nothing that could stop tanks or aircraft. They retreated. | 28 June: North Korea captured Seoul, the capital of South Korea. | Within weeks, North Korea had control of most of the South. |
|---|---|---|---|

## Now try this

'Kim Il-Sung was the main reason for the Korean War.' Give **two** points that support this statement, and **two** points that argue against it. For each point, explain your thinking.

You could refer back to page 4 to help you answer this question.

# Responses to invasion

North Korea's invasion of South Korea produced an immediate response from the USA and the UN. This threatened to turn the invasion into an international crisis. The USSR's response was complicated by US relations with China.

## Responses to the invasion of South Korea, 25 June 1950

**The US response**

President Truman was determined to contain the spread of communism. Truman:
- immediately ordered US Navy forces to Korea (the 7th Fleet)
- ordered **General MacArthur** to organise troops and supplies to send to South Korea
- put pressure on the United Nations to take military action against North Korea.

**The USSR's absence from the UN**

The USSR could have used its **veto** to prevent the UN acting against North Korea. However:
- The USA would not allow communist China to join the UN's Security Council.
- As a result, the USSR was refusing to take part in the discussions of the UN.
- This meant the USSR was absent from the Security Council meeting to block the vote.

The USSR criticised the UN's plans, saying the UN was following US orders. The USSR had misjudged the USA's determination to defend South Korea.

**The United Nations' response**

The UN Security Council met on 25 June to decide its response.
- It agreed that North Korea had broken world peace and called for a ceasefire, ordering Kim to withdraw his troops back to the border on the 38th parallel.
- On 27 June, the USA insisted that the UN must send its army to defend South Korea. The Security Council agreed.

For information on the Truman Doctrine and the UN Security Council, see page 2.

As a permanent member of the UN's Security Council, the USSR had the power to veto UN resolutions. This meant that it could block or stop a UN decision from being put into action, but only if it took part in the discussions.

## The United Nations forces

- ✓ 16 UN countries sent troops and five sent medical support.
- ✓ The USA provided 50% of the UN troops and 90% of the navy and air forces.
- ✓ The UN's forces were led by the United Nations Command (UNC). Americans were put in charge of the UNC.
- ✓ General MacArthur, an American war hero from the Second World War, was put in charge of the UN forces and the armed forces of South Korea.

In 1950, South Korea had 92 000 troops; North Korea had 135 000.

## Reasons for the USA's response

Here are three key reasons for the USA's response to the invasion of South Korea:

 1 The South Korean forces could not stop the North Koreans on their own.

2 After the 'loss' of China to communism, President Truman needed to show tough commitment to containing its further spread. 'McCarthyism' was stirring up fear of communist influence within the USA itself.

3 The USA suspected that the USSR was using Korea as a diversion. Involving other UN countries in Korea would make sure the USA was free to act against the USSR in Europe.

For more on McCarthy, see page 3.

Write a paragraph to explain why the USSR was absent from the United Nations in June 1950. What consequence did this have for the UN's response to the crisis in Korea?

# The UN campaign in the South and North

By September 1950, Northern forces had pushed the South's forces into a small area around the city of Pusan (now called Busan). By November, the UN campaign had pushed the Northern forces back towards the border with China.

## The four stages of the Korean War

The UN's campaign was so successful that the USA changed its objectives from containing communism to pushing it back. China's response to this had serious consequences for the UN campaign and for Korea.

 North Korea invades South Korea, 25 June 1950.

 The UN's Inchon landings on 15 September lead to the recapture of South Korea. UN forces advance into North Korea.

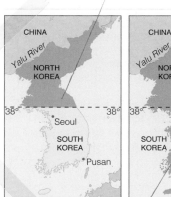  

 By September 1950, the North has captured most of South Korea.

 In October 1950, China's response pushes the UN back into South Korea, leading to military stalemate along the 38th parallel.

## The UN campaign in South Korea

UN troops from the USA and Australia were the first to arrive in South Korea in September 1950. The situation was very bad.

- The South Korean army (92 000 men) had been forced back to a 100-square mile area around the southern port of Pusan. North Korea's forces (135 000 men) controlled almost everywhere else.

- At first, the UN troops were not well equipped. They had old Second World War weapons and equipment. They were new recruits, without fighting experience.

- The North Korean troops were very well equipped with modern Soviet weapons. Most had fought with the Red Army in China's civil war: they were experienced troops.

- The South had defended Pusan from three attacks in August. The UN forces were nearly defeated by a huge attack on 1 September. However, the North's forces suffered major losses in the process.

## The Inchon landings

General MacArthur had perfected **amphibious assaults** during the Second World War. He used this strategy of invading enemy territory from the sea to achieve an outstanding victory.

- The amphibious assault of 15 September 1950 attacked the port city of Inchon, near Seoul, with the North weak from fighting.

- This attack was extremely risky because of Inchon's strong natural defences, for example high cliffs and strong tides.

- The assault (300 ships, 70 000 fresh men) took North Korea by surprise and UN troops quickly captured Inchon and an important nearby airfield.

- From this base, the UN launched its attack on Seoul. Ten days later, Seoul was freed.

- At the same time, the UN led a 'breakout' from Pusan. The North Koreans were trapped between two forces. Although many escaped, perhaps 40 000 were killed or captured. South Korea was recaptured.

### Now try this

'The Inchon landings were the most important event of the Korean War.' Using the maps to help you, give **two** points that support this statement and **two** points that argue against it.

# Advance into North Korea

After the successful UN campaign to recapture South Korea, on 1 October 1950 the first UN forces advanced into the North. By 20 October, UN forces had captured the capital, Pyongyang.

## Reasons for the UN advance

The UN had successfully defended South Korea from North Korea. So why did the UN forces cross the 38th parallel on 1 October 1950? Here are three key reasons:

1. Around 35 000 North Korean troops had escaped back to North Korea. These troops might attack the South again in the future if they were not chased down and defeated.

2. Truman hoped to win an impressive victory against communism and reunite Korea under a government that was friendly to the USA.

3. Truman's military advisers, including MacArthur, were certain that the USSR and China would not join the war. They hadn't joined the war when North Korea had almost won: why would they join it now it was facing defeat?

## The UN advance into the North

### Timeline

**3 October** China warns that it will enter the war if the USA or UN crosses the 38th parallel.

**9 October** The US Eighth Army also crosses the 38th parallel.

**19 October** US and ROK troops take North Korea's capital city, Pyongyang. North Korean troops retreat into the mountains.

**1 October 1950** ROK (Republic of Korea) troops cross the 38th parallel into North Korea.

**7 October** The UN passes a resolution calling for the unification of Korea.

**15 October** General MacArthur assures President Truman that China will not intervene.

**25 October** A few units of ROK troops reach the Yalu River: the border between North Korea and China.

## UN air superiority

The USA was confident that China would not join the war in October 1950 because the US could provide massive air support to the UN troops.

☑ US aeroplanes had total control of the skies over North Korea, because North Korea had few air defences.

☑ Any movement of troops over the Chinese border would therefore have to face devastating US bombing attacks.

This photograph from 1 October 1950 shows the first UN troops to cross the 38th parallel into North Korea. These were South Korean troops (ROK) with their US advisers.

## An extract from the UN Security Council's Resolution 84, 5 July 1950

The Security Council recommends that Members of the United Nations provide 'such assistance to the Republic of Korea [South Korea] as may be necessary to repel the armed attack [by forces from North Korea] and to restore international peace and security in the area'.

The USA said that it would only be possible to 'restore international peace and security' in the area by going into North Korea, because otherwise North Korea would attack the South again.

The UN had agreed in July 1950 to help South Korea repel the attack by North Korea. **Repel** means to push away or make something go away.

### Now try this

Look at the extract from the UN Security Council's Resolution 84 above. What message do you think it gives about the UN's aims in Korea in July 1950? Is it clear? Explain your answer in a short paragraph.

# China's reaction

Although US military experts were confident China would not fight to defend North Korea, they were wrong. On 25 October 1950, a massive Chinese attack pushed the UN forces back into the South, widening the conflict further.

## China's warning

After ROK troops crossed the border at the 38th parallel on 1 October 1950, China sent a warning that it would intervene if US or UN troops came into North Korea. Because China was not allowed into the UN, it had to send this message through its Indian ambassador.

## China's preparation for war

In mid-October 1950, 300 000 soldiers from China's Communist Party Volunteers Army Corps (CPV) moved secretly into the mountains of North Korea and camouflaged their positions so they were very hard to spot from the air. Then they waited for the right time to attack.

This Chinese drawing from 1951 celebrates Chinese soldiers joining North Korean forces. Note the dead US soldier, modern Soviet weapons and the difficult mountain terrain.

See Map 4 on page 7 for more on the stalemate.

## Intervention of Chinese troops

On 25 October, the Chinese forces attacked.

- UN divisions had pushed into North Korea too quickly. The Chinese forces moved behind them and cut them off.
- At first, General MacArthur refused to allow any UN troops to retreat from the North. This made the situation even worse.
- By 28 November, UN troops were fleeing from the attacking Chinese.
- The Chinese and North Korean forces swept southwards, pushing the UN forces back into South Korea. Seoul was captured.
- By spring 1951, UN forces had recaptured Seoul but were stuck in a **stalemate** along the 38th parallel.

## Consequences of China's reaction

1 US troops suffered heavy casualties and were defeated in battle for the first time. This affected US public support for the war.

2 China succeeded in defending North Korea. Truman chose to accept containment instead of pushing communism back, saying that the war must be limited to Korea.

3 On 11 April 1951, General MacArthur was sacked because he refused to obey Truman's orders not to send troops back into North Korea. MacArthur had also argued for attacking China and for using atomic bombs.

4 Soviet MiG-15 fighters, whose pilots pretended to be Chinese or Korean, countered US air superiority over Korea.

WORLD WAR III IN ASIA

NOT A GENERAL'S JOB

This US political cartoon was published on 10 April 1951. It shows MacArthur attempting to lever a hat representing the USA off a cliff labelled 'World War III in Asia'.

## Now try this

1 Look at the image of Chinese and North Korean troops greeting each other. Identify **two** things that are useful about this source for understanding why the UN's advance was defeated.

2 The US political cartoon is critical of General MacArthur. Write a paragraph to explain what it is criticising MacArthur for.

# Stalemate and peace talks

By mid-1951, a stalemate had been reached. Peace talks began, but the war continued until 1953, when a new US president, Eisenhower, took office and Stalin, the USSR's leader, died.

## Key events in the Korean War

**Timeline**

**15 September 1950** Inchon landings.

**26–30 November 1950** Chinese push UN forces out of North Korea.

**14 March 1951** UN forces recapture Seoul.

**11 April 1951** General MacArthur is sacked.

**August 1951** Peace talks break down.

**December 1951** Communists end air attacks.

**May–July 1953** USA intensifies air war. More than 150 MiG-15s shot down by US fighters.

**25 June 1950** Invasion of South Korea.

**20 October 1950** UN forces capture Pyongyang.

**4 January 1951** UN forces lose control of Seoul.

**Spring 1951** Stalemate begins as both sides fortify their lines along the 38th parallel. Heavy Chinese losses: 85 000 casualties.

**July 1951** Peace talks begin.

**September 1951** The air war begins.

**29 August 1952** Biggest UN air raid of the war kills 6000 North Koreans in Pyongyang.

**27 July 1953** Armistice (end of fighting) agreement is signed to end the war.

## Peace talks

As the war reached stalemate in the spring of 1951, both sides tried to find a way to end the conflict. But there were major difficulties in:

- agreeing where the border would be between North and South Korea
- agreeing how the return of prisoners of war would be handled (16 000 Chinese prisoners did not want to go back to communist China)
- deciding what would happen to Chinese forces and UN forces (the USA wanted to keep its forces in South Korea to defend it).

## Military stalemate around the 38th parallel

- To force North Korea to accept peace terms, the USA bombed targets in the North. Up to one million North Koreans were killed. US air attacks used **napalm**.
- North Korea and China asked the USSR for support. The USSR provided MiG-15 jet fighter aeroplanes: the best in the world. An air war resulted. The USA lost 3500 aeroplanes early in the air war, challenging its air superiority for several months. North Korea and China lost 3000 aeroplanes.
- After May 1953, the UN intensified attacks. US bombers destroyed dams, causing terrible damage to North Korea's farming.

For more on napalm, see page 20.

## Reasons for the end of the war

1. After the death of Stalin, neither China nor North Korea could be sure if Soviet help would continue.
2. The intensification of the USA's bombing of North Korea in 1953 meant the country struggled to feed its people.
3. China was beginning its first Five-Year Plan to industrialise the country. It needed to reduce military spending to do this.

## The armistice and end of the war

On 27 July 1953, a ceasefire agreement was signed by North Korea, China and the UN. North and South Korea remained divided, at the 38th parallel. Despite the end of the conflict, tension between the two countries continued.

A 3 km-wide demilitarised zone (DMZ) was set up between the two countries. The aim of the DMZ was to prevent the two sides coming into contact with each other and triggering further conflict.

**Now try this**

By spring 1951, the fighting in the Korean War had reached a stalemate. Write an account of the events that led to the war becoming an international crisis.

Look back at pages 4–9 to help you.

# Korean War: impact

The Korean War had a significant impact on Korea, on the UN and on Sino-American relations (China and the USA). It also had consequences for further conflict and tension in Asia.

## Impact on Korea

- Korea remained divided. This was distressing for Koreans, especially those whose families were split up by the North–South divide.
- Both North and South Korea were left in ruins by the war. North Korea rebuilt quickly thanks to Soviet aid. South Korea struggled to develop at first because of the corrupt and restrictive government under President Rhee, but massive US aid helped it recover.
- Deaths: estimates of 200 000 soldiers and one million civilians from the South, perhaps 400 000 soldiers and 600 000 civilians from the North. (There are no accurate records.) This was over 10% of North Korea's total population!

## Impact on the United Nations

- The Korean War showed that the UN was a powerful organisation for tackling world peace.
- The UN succeeded in defending South Korea, at a cost of nearly 40 000 UN lives.
- The UN was criticised by the USSR for doing what the USA told it to. However, the USSR did rejoin the UN.

## Impact on Sino-American relations

- Relations between the USA and China got worse. The USA had organised a ban on trade with China in 1950 that was tightened in 1952.
- The USA continued to support a rival Chinese government based in Taiwan. US military defence stopped communist China from eliminating the threat from Taiwan.
- The Korean War made the USA very cautious about China's reaction in the Vietnam War that followed (1955–1975).

For more information on the escalation of the Vietnam War, see pages 12–15 and page 23.

## Impact on the Cold War

The Korean War had important consequences for Cold War conflict and tension.

- 36 500 US troops died in Korea. This had a negative impact on public opinion and made the USA cautious about sending US troops into other foreign conflicts.
- It showed both the USA and the USSR that they could fight in a limited way (not involving nuclear weapons) through conflicts between other countries.
- The USA was convinced that the USSR was spreading communism in Asia. Eisenhower started funding France's war in **Indochina** because of the high risk of further countries falling to communism.

Indochina – a French colony, made up of modern-day Vietnam, Cambodia and Laos.

### The Korean War: key statistics

- ✓ The USA spent around $20–30 billion on the war in Korea (about $340 billion today).
- ✓ US planes dropped about 635 000 tons of bombs on North Korea (more than that used in the Pacific, 1941–1945). US pilots sometimes reported that there were no more targets left standing to bomb.
- ✓ Over 1000 British Commonwealth troops died in the Korean War, 710 from the UK.
- ✓ It is estimated that there were 72 000 Soviets in North Korea, including hundreds of pilots. The USSR kept this a secret in case it triggered war with the USA.

Some sources give the number of US deaths in Korea as 54 000. This figure is actually all US combat deaths between 1950 and 1953 around the world.

## Now try this

'The Korean War was a disaster for the Korean people.' Give **two** points that support this view and **two** points you could use to argue against it.

# End of French rule

Vietnam was part of a French colony known as Indochina, lost to Japan in the Second World War. After Japan's defeat in 1945, France tried to take back control of Vietnam. The **Vietminh** wanted Vietnam to be independent – and communist. So, the **First Indochina War** began.

## The end of French colonial rule

**Timeline**

**September 1940** Japan occupies Vietnam.

**June 1940** France surrenders to Nazi Germany.

**1941 Ho Chi Minh** creates the **Vietminh**: the League for the Independence of Vietnam. They lead the fight for Vietnamese independence.

**1944–1945** Two million Vietnamese die in a famine. The Vietminh organise famine relief.

**August 1945** Japan surrenders. The Vietminh take control of most of Vietnam.

**2 September 1945** Ho Chi Minh, leader of the Vietminh, declares Vietnam is independent.

**September 1945** French troops fight the Vietminh as France tries to take back control.

**December 1946** First Indochina War begins.

**1949** Communists win China's civil war. China begins supporting the Vietminh.

**1950** The USA begins supporting France in Vietnam.

**1953** French losses in the war reach 100 000 deaths. The war is very unpopular in France.

**April 1954** US President Eisenhower describes the **Domino Theory** in a speech.

**May 1954** The French lose the **Battle of Dien Bien Phu**: French troops surrender.

**July 1954 Geneva Conference** ends war and agrees peace accords; French Indochina is broken up and Vietnam temporarily **divided**.

For information on Dien Bien Phu and the Geneva Agreement, see page 13.

## Reasons for the end of French rule

There are three key reasons for the end of French colonial rule in Vietnam.

**1 French colonial rule was unfair and oppressive.** For example, France took Vietnam's raw materials and sold them to make France richer. Vietnamese workers were beaten to make them work harder. As a result, people like Ho Chi Minh were determined to make Vietnam independent of foreign rule. They had struggled against French colonial rule for many years.

**2 France lost control of Vietnam to the Japanese in the Second World War.** Japan's occupation of Vietnam included executing thousands of French officers. As a result, when Japan surrendered, French troops were too weak to stop the Vietminh taking control.

**3 The Vietminh's communism meant support from communist China.** For example, Chinese military advisers trained Vietminh troops into a very effective army of 300 000. As a result, France could not defeat them, leading to surrender at Dien Bien Phu.

## US involvement in Vietnam

- Usually the USA supported countries that wanted independence from colonial rule. Ho Chi Minh hoped the USA would help him.

- However, China and North Korea were already communist. The USA was very worried that, if Vietnam became communist, other countries would become communist too, such as Cambodia or Laos.

- France was able to get US support for its war because France argued that it was a war against a communist dictatorship.

As a result, by 1953, the USA was paying for nearly 80% of France's war in Vietnam.

**Now try this**

Write a short paragraph to explain the main reason why the USA became involved in France's war against the Vietminh.

# Dien Bien Phu

French forces were defeated by the Vietminh at the Battle of Dien Bien Phu in May 1954. As a result, peace talks were held to end the First French Indochina War. These led to the Geneva Agreement in July 1954, which divided Vietnam.

## Why were the French at Dien Bien Phu?

The French built a fortified base and airstrip at Dien Bien Phu as part of a plan to trick the Vietminh into an open battle. They brought in 11 000 troops. The French assumed they would beat the Vietminh because of their superior military strength.

The French believed they had superior weapons and tactics. They never imagined that they would be surrounded by artillery and anti-aircraft guns.

The French base was surrounded by jungle-covered hills. Vietminh General Giap moved 200 artillery guns into the hills. (Giap and Ho Chi Minh led the Vietminh together.) The French base became a trap with no way out.

General Giap secretly moved 50 000 men and his artillery up narrow mountain tracks, and then camouflaged his forces so they could not be spotted by aeroplanes.

**Superior Vietminh tactics**

The French did not think it was possible to bring artillery into such a mountainous area where there were no real roads.

**Over-confident French tactics**

### Reasons for the French defeat at Dien Bien Phu, May 1954

The Vietminh had been very well trained. Their artillery gunners could fire 50 shells a minute – a devastating rate of fire that smashed the French base and airstrip.

**Support from the local population**

**Support from China**

Dien Bien Phu was located in a remote northern region. The French assumed they would be able to fly in supplies, but supply aeroplanes were shot down by anti-aircraft guns.

240 000 civilians carried everything needed for the Vietminh attack, including the disassembled big guns. They travelled on foot, up miles of narrow trails into the hills.

China provided guns and ammunition, training for Vietminh troops and military advice, and 20 000 bikes to help locals move supplies.

## Consequences of Dien Bien Phu

- On 7 May 1954, the French surrendered. 8000 French troops had been killed or wounded in 55 days of constant attacks.
- As a result, the French prime minister resigned. The French parliament voted to end the war and leave Vietnam.
- The Geneva Agreement was made between France and Indochinese representatives in 1954. The USA, however, did not sign the agreement.
- The victory over the French made Ho Chi Minh and General Giap national heroes.

## Five results of the 1954 Geneva Agreement

1. Vietnam was temporarily divided into North Vietnam and South Vietnam.
2. Ho Chi Minh would lead North Vietnam. US-backed politician Ngo Dinh Diem would lead South Vietnam.
3. The French would leave Vietnam and the Vietminh would leave South Vietnam.
4. Vietnamese people could decide whether they wanted to live in the North or South.
5. A general election would be held by 1956 to decide who led a reunited Vietnam. Ho Chi Minh looked likely to win this election.

## Now try this

Once you've read through this page, cover it up and list:
a) **four** reasons for the French defeat at Dien Bien Phu
b) **four** consequences of Dien Bien Phu.

# Civil war in South Vietnam

The Geneva Agreement meant that, in 1955, Ngo Dinh Diem became the leader of South Vietnam – until an election for the whole of Vietnam could be held. When Diem refused to allow this election, his decision helped trigger a civil war in South Vietnam.

## Ngo Dinh Diem's rise to power

Diem was from a Catholic family, in a mainly Buddhist country. His father's family had suffered violent anti-Catholic persecution from Buddhists.

In 1945, Diem was captured by the Vietminh. He refused to join Ho Chi Minh's government and went into self-imposed exile.

In 1950, Diem travelled to the USA, hoping to get US backing to lead Vietnam. Political leaders were impressed by his anti-communist beliefs.

Ngo Dinh Diem and his two brothers, one of whom was a Catholic bishop.

In 1954, Diem became prime minister of South Vietnam. For a year he fought other non-communist rivals who wanted to lead the country.

In 1955, a referendum took place in South Vietnam to decide who should be leader: Diem or his rival, Bo Dai. Bo Dai was the leader of South Vietnam appointed by the French. Diem cheated in order to win the vote, claiming 98.2% chose him as President of the Republic of Vietnam.

## What caused the civil war?

Diem's actions were the main cause of the war.

- He refused to allow elections to decide who should lead a unified Vietnam – because he was likely to lose to Ho Chi Minh.
- Diem's security forces arrested people who campaigned against this decision. They also targeted anyone known to be a communist or who complained about government corruption.
- His favouritism towards Catholics alienated the mostly Buddhist population.

- Thousands of Diem's political opponents were executed and tens of thousands jailed.
- By 1957, opponents of Diem's leadership began an armed **insurgency** (rebellion) against Diem and his supporters.
- In 1959, North Vietnamese leaders agreed to support the opponents of Diem's regime.

## The civil war – NLF vs ARVN

**The National Liberation Front (NLF)**
- Created by North Vietnam's leaders in 1960 to combat Diem and unify (join together) Vietnam.
- Fighters often were South Vietnamese Vietminh. Many had relocated to North Vietnam but were sent back home to fight.
- Supplied by North Vietnam through the Ho Chi Minh Trail, named after the North Vietnamese leader.

For more on the Ho Chi Minh Trail, see page 20.

**The Army of the Republic of Vietnam (ARVN)**
- Created by Diem in 1955 as part of his setting up of the new Republic of Vietnam (South Vietnam).
- The ARVN was a modern army, supported by the USA with money and equipment.
- Used by Diem to defend his regime from communists (NLF) and non-communist opponents, for example Buddhist groups.

## Now try this

Write **one** sentence to describe each of the following:
a) the ARVN; b) the NLF; c) Ho Chi Minh; d) the Republic of Vietnam (RVN); e) Ngo Dinh Diem; f) Bo Dai.

# Opposition to Diem

Diem's unpopular government was corrupt. Its treatment of peasants and Buddhists caused tension and conflict. Opposition to his rule made it difficult for the USA to keep supporting him.

**Persecution of communists**
Diem's 'Denunciation of Communists' campaign (1955–1959) arrested, imprisoned and executed thousands. His 'Law 10/59' (1959) meant military courts could execute anyone found guilty of belonging to a communist organisation – for example, the Vietminh.

**Corruption**
Diem and his family used their power to make money for themselves by taking over businesses and controlling trade.

**Nepotism**
Diem appointed family members and supporters to important government positions (this is known as nepotism). It created a dictatorship because his government did whatever Diem told them to.

**Resettlement of peasants**
Diem's 'Agroville' programme resettled peasants from their villages to areas under government control. Often the peasants were forced to move.

**Persecution of Buddhists**
Catholics had important roles in government under French rule. This continued under Diem's leadership, and Diem began to persecute other religions. In May 1963, nine Buddhists were shot dead during demonstrations after Diem's government banned religious flags.

**Reasons for opposition to Diem**

In June 1963, Buddhist monk **Thich Quang Duc** set himself on fire to protest Diem's persecution of Buddhists. His protest sparked international criticism of Diem.

## Why did the USA stop supporting Diem?

- For most of Diem's rule (1954–1963), the USA sent money to help redevelop South Vietnam. They knew Diem kept a lot of this money for himself and his supporters.
- The USA sent military support to help the ARVN fight communists. But the ARVN seemed unable to make progress. In 1963, the ARVN were defeated by NLF troops at the battle of Ap Bac, despite having US military advisers, US helicopters and US M113 armoured personnel carriers.
- The persecution of Buddhists in 1963 caused the USA to stop its support. Thich Quang Duc's protest was worldwide news. There was massive international criticism of Diem's brutality. Public opinion made US support impossible.

## Consequences of opposition to Diem

1. **Civil war** – Diem's government seemed just as unfair and exploiting as French colonial rule had been. Fighting Diem was the same as fighting for Vietnamese independence to many people.
2. **Negative view of the USA** – Diem's regime only survived because of US support. This meant many South Vietnamese thought that the USA was helping to oppress them.
3. **Tension in the USA** – Some Americans felt it was wrong to support Diem's corrupt regime, because the USA should be helping build democracy, independence and freedom, not propping up a corrupt dictatorship.
4. **Increased US involvement** – In November 1963, Diem was forced out and killed. This caused political chaos in South Vietnam, making it even weaker. The USA increased its involvement, fearing a communist takeover.

**Now try this**

Once you have revised this page, close the book and try to recreate the spider diagram. Aim to include **five** reasons for opposition to Diem.

# The Vietcong

The Vietcong was the name given by Diem's regime to the resistance fighters who rose up against his unpopular regime after his refusal to allow elections uniting the North and South. Their aim was to overthrow Diem and unite Vietnam as an independent country.

## What were the aims of the Vietcong?

The Vietcong was set up by Ho Chi Minh and other North Vietnamese leaders in December 1960. It brought together different groups fighting against Diem's regime in South Vietnam.

The Vietcong's aims were:

- to overthrow Diem's corrupt regime and replace it with a fair government
- to join North and South Vietnam together again as one independent country, free from foreign control
- to stop the oppression of peasants by taking land from rich landlords and giving it to the peasants, and ending Diem's increased taxes on them.

Vietcong fighters were forbidden from mistreating peasants by their leaders. The Vietcong relied on peasant support.

## Support for the Vietcong

- Many Vietcong were communist supporters, but others were not. For example, the leader of the Vietcong – Hua Tho – was not a communist.
- Although many Vietcong came from the South, North Vietnam's support was crucial: for fighters, equipment and money.
- Support for the Vietcong from China and the USSR also came down from the North.
- Peasants in South Vietnam liked the land reform promised by the Vietcong, and many supported their fighters. Others were forced to support the Vietcong – for example, by giving them their food.

### Leadership of the Vietcong

Ho Chi Minh's victories against the Japanese and the French inspired many Vietcong to fight for independence. His inspirational role was very important to the Vietcong.

## Vietcong tactics

The Vietcong used **terror tactics**, especially assassinations and bombings, to attack Diem's regime. They targeted government officials and foreigners, but innocent civilians were often hurt or killed, too.

The Vietcong used **guerrilla tactics**, including:

- **Ambushes:** Vietcong fighters used stealth skills to enter an area, hide themselves completely then wait patiently for a coordinated surprise attack.
- **Sabotage:** by destroying bridges and equipment, the Vietcong made it more difficult for the ARVN to operate.
- **Spying:** getting information about enemy targets and weaknesses.
- **Using the local population:** local people fed and sheltered Vietcong. The Vietcong dressed the same as local people, so the ARVN could never be sure who might attack them or who had attacked them.

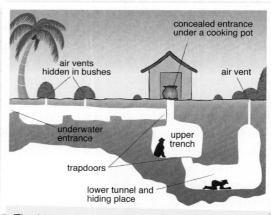

The Vietcong used tunnel systems to launch ambushes. The ARVN searched villages for Vietcong by looking for weapons or extra food, so these were also hidden in tunnels.

Although the Vietcong usually avoided open battles, there were battles between the Vietcong and the ARVN. Ap Bac in January 1963 is a good example. 300 Vietcong defeated 1500 ARVN, killing 100 ARVN soldiers and three US advisers.

## Now try this

Describe **two** ways in which Vietcong tactics made it hard for the ARVN to defeat them.

# The Domino Theory

The USA was determined to stop communism spreading from one country to another. This was the main reason why the USA became involved in the conflict in South Vietnam.

## Containment

After the Second World War, the USSR spread communist control throughout Eastern Europe. The USA decided on a policy to contain communism.

- In 1947, President Truman said the USA would help any country resist takeover by communists: the Truman Doctrine.
- First, the USA funded European governments who were fighting civil wars against communists, for example Greece.
- Then, in 1950, the USA sent troops to Korea. This was, at first, to stop communism spreading to the South, then to push back communism in North Korea. This ended when China joined the war.

For more on containment and the Truman Doctrine, see pages 1–2.

US concerns about the spread of communism included the fear that communists would take control of the USA. US politician Joseph McCarthy led a campaign to root out US communists. Fear about US communists increased the pressure to contain the spread of communism worldwide.

## The Domino Theory

In 1954, US President Eisenhower described the situation in Asia as being like a line of dominoes: if one country fell to communism, many others would quickly follow.

The **Domino Theory** was a reaction to the spread of communism to China. The USA had supported a nationalist government against communists in China's civil war, but the communists won. US politicians felt they had 'lost' China to communism.

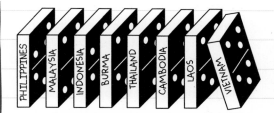

The Domino Theory predicted that eight Asian countries were vulnerable to the spread of communism.

## Consequences of the Domino Theory

The USA only became involved in Vietnam in order to contain communism in Asia.

- The USA supported Diem's corrupt dictatorship because he was strongly anti-communist. The USA also shared Diem's reluctance for a democratic election in Vietnam, because communist Ho Chi Minh seemed certain to win.
- When the Diem regime collapsed in 1963, South Vietnam was seriously weakened. The USA increased its involvement to try to stabilise South Vietnam and keep up the pressure on the Vietcong.

## Limitations of US involvement

Although the USA increased its involvement in Vietnam in 1963, there were important limits.

- After the loss of 36 500 American lives in the Korean War, the US public did not want US troops in another conflict in Asia.
- China and North Vietnam were allies. Attacks on North Vietnam risked bringing China into the war. This had happened in Korea, with very negative consequences.
- The USA and the USSR had only just avoided nuclear war over the Soviet placement of missiles on communist Cuba in 1962. Attacks on North Vietnam risked bringing the USSR into this war as well, as an ally of China and North Vietnam.

## Now try this

Write a paragraph to explain the connection between the Domino Theory and US involvement in Vietnam.

# Eisenhower and Kennedy

US presidents Eisenhower and Kennedy both wanted to keep the USA's role in Vietnam limited to funding and military advice. But, as the Vietcong grew stronger, US involvement increased.

## US intervention under Eisenhower, 1953–1961

Eisenhower believed the Domino Theory, but limited US involvement to avoid war with China. The USA sent money to help Diem develop South Vietnam and sent around 700 military advisers to help the ARVN beat the Vietcong.

**1960:** Eisenhower urges Diem to use land reform to increase his popularity. Diem ignores this advice.

| | | | | |
|---|---|---|---|---|
| **1954:** South East Asia Treaty Organisation (SEATO) founded: eight countries working to defend Asia from communism. | **1955:** The US-run referendum is won by Diem. Diem cheats and claims 98.2% of votes. | **1956:** Diem refuses to allow elections. | **1957:** Oppression of Diem's opponents. US support continues. | By the end of 1960, less than half of South Vietnam is under government control. |

→ US involvement in Vietnam under Eisenhower

## US intervention under Kennedy, 1961–1963

Like Eisenhower, Kennedy also wanted to avoid the USA getting directly involved in the fighting. However, it was clear that the ARVN were losing the civil war. This situation had to be tackled.

- The ARVN had been trying to get the Vietcong to fight open battles, but instead were worn down by guerrilla tactics. Kennedy sent thousands more military advisers to work alongside ARVN troops and train them in a new strategy: hunt down Vietcong cells (small groups) in the countryside and eliminate them.

- Opposition to Diem meant the Vietcong had a lot of support. Kennedy wanted a new '**hearts and minds**' strategy to win support for Diem's government. US advisers would help peasants to defend their villages from the Vietcong.

For more on opposition to Diem and the Agroville programme, see page 15.

## The Strategic Hamlets programme, 1962

Diem's 'Agrovilles' aimed to get peasants away from the Vietcong and into areas that the government could control. US advisers supported this idea and it developed into the **Strategic Hamlets programme**.

- Strategic hamlets were large new villages with facilities, such as schools, surrounded by defences such as spiked bamboo fences and guarded by the ARVN.

- 800 US advisers helped the ARVN to set up 5000 new strategic hamlets.

- However, many peasants had to be forced to leave their old villages, which were often burnt down. People hated leaving ancestors' graves, which were spiritually important.

- Vietcong attacks on the strategic hamlets often easily overcame the ARVN defences.

- Resentment against the programme increased opposition to Diem by 300%!

## Increased involvement: facts and figures

- ✓ **1961:** $136 million sent in economic aid, plus $65 million in military equipment and $40 million to train ARVN.
- ✓ **1961:** 300 US helicopters and pilots sent to Vietnam to transport ARVN troops.
- ✓ **1963:** Number of US military advisers in Vietnam increased to 16 000.

## Kennedy and Diem's overthrow

In November 1963, a group of ARVN generals plotted to overthrow Diem. When the USA found out about this, senior officials secretly told the generals that the USA would not try to stop them. However, Kennedy was very upset when Diem and his brother were then murdered by soldiers.

**Now try this**

Identify **two** pieces of evidence of how US involvement in Vietnam increased from 1953 to 1963.

# The Gulf of Tonkin incident

Under President Johnson (1963–1969), the conflict in Vietnam escalated dramatically. The Gulf of Tonkin incident in 1964 was key to increased US intervention in Vietnam.

## Events leading to the Gulf of Tonkin Resolution, 1964

US and ARVN special forces carried out secret missions in the Gulf of Tonkin (east of North Vietnam), sabotaging North Vietnamese facilities and collecting information on North Vietnam.

On 31 July 1964, ARVN commandos attacked a North Vietnamese radar station. A US warship, the *USS Maddox*, was monitoring these radar stations in the Gulf of Tonkin.

On 2 August 1964, North Vietnamese torpedo boats fired on the *USS Maddox*. One torpedo hit but did not explode. The *USS Maddox* and US fighter planes sank two torpedo boats.

On 4 August 1964, a second attack was reported by the *USS Maddox*, later shown to be a mistake made by panicky sailors. No attack actually took place.

President Johnson ordered the US air force to attack North Vietnamese gunboat bases. Many were destroyed. Johnson told the US public that the USA faced open aggression from North Vietnam.

The US Congress had previously been strongly against the USA getting more involved in Vietnam. But, after the Gulf of Tonkin incident, Congress was outraged.

On 7 August 1964, Johnson took the Gulf of Tonkin Resolution to Congress. This gave the president the power to defend US forces and South Vietnam in whatever way he thought best. Congress passed the resolution almost unanimously and it was signed on 10 August.

Johnson signs the Gulf of Tonkin Resolution, 10 August 1964. This gave him the power to escalate the war in Vietnam following the Gulf of Tonkin incident without consulting Congress – which meant he was able to overcome the previous lack of support for the war from Congress.

## Why did Johnson increase US involvement?

Johnson increased US involvement in Vietnam in reaction to the Gulf of Tonkin incident because:

**1** Following Diem's removal, the Vietcong had increased from 23 000 fighters in 1963 to 60 000 in 1964.

**2** There was a US presidential election in 1964. Johnson's opponent criticised him for not being tough enough in Vietnam. (After the Gulf of Tonkin Resolution, Johnson won the election very easily.)

**3** Johnson's military advisers were certain that, if the USA bombed North Vietnam from the air, North Vietnam would soon stop supporting the Vietcong.

### Johnson and the Gulf of Tonkin Resolution

Because the second attack on the *USS Maddox* was not real, some historians are critical of the Gulf of Tonkin Resolution. They suggest that Congress was tricked into giving Johnson the power to escalate the USA's involvement.

It is true that Johnson had the resolution ready for two months before August 1964. He waited for the right opportunity to bring it to Congress in order to increase US intervention. However, at the time, the sailors involved were convinced an attack was happening.

---

**Now try this**

'The purpose of the Gulf of Tonkin Resolution was to allow the use of US military power to force North Vietnam to give up its aim of uniting Vietnam.' Give **one** point supporting this statement, and **one** point that argues against it.

# The mass bombing campaign

The Gulf of Tonkin incident gave the US military the opportunity to tackle the war in new ways, to try to respond to Vietcong tactics. One was to make more use of US airpower: mass bombing.

For more on Vietcong tactics, see page 16.

## The problem: North Vietnamese support

US military advisers believed that the Vietcong relied on support from the North:

- Thousands of North Vietnamese were sent south to train Vietcong groups.
- The Vietcong gained high-quality weapons from North Vietnam, including AK-47s.
- Sometimes whole North Vietnamese army units joined Vietcong divisions.
- These troops and supplies used the Ho Chi Minh Trail: a 16 000 km network of paths from North to South Vietnam.

## The problem: The Ho Chi Minh Trail

Much of the Ho Chi Minh Trail ran through neutral countries: Laos and Cambodia.

## US response: Operation Rolling Thunder

In March 1965, the USA began a mass bombing campaign called **Operation Rolling Thunder**. This aimed to:

- convince North Vietnam to stop supporting the Vietcong
- destroy the industries and transport links that were sending supplies to the south.

Expected to succeed in eight weeks, the campaign lasted three years. By November 1968, nearly 900 000 tons of bombs had been dropped, killing 90 000 people.

## US response: mass bombing

The USA used bombing to try to disrupt the flow of traffic along the Ho Chi Minh Trail.

- US aeroplanes sprayed defoliant chemicals, such as Agent Orange, which destroyed plants to reveal the paths in the forest.
- Once troop movements were spotted, **cluster bombs** and **napalm** were dropped from aeroplanes to kill large numbers. Cluster bombs broke into many different bomblets, spreading out over a wider area. Napalm was petroleum jelly set on fire. The burning napalm was effective at killing people because it stuck to skin.

## How effective was the US response?

- Operation Rolling Thunder could not target areas that might bring China into the war, like the port of Haiphong, used by Chinese ships. Most of the supplies for the Vietcong came in from China.
- The USA underestimated the North Vietnamese people. Thousands worked to repair damage, no matter how frequent.
- China and the USSR supplied North Vietnam with very sophisticated air defences. 745 US airmen were shot down.

## How effective was the US response?

- The Vietcong built hundreds of carefully hidden underground bases along the Ho Chi Minh Trail to shelter from US air strikes.
- Thousands of Vietcong constantly repaired and improved the trail. More supplies made it along the trail than before, and the route got quicker – in the end it took just six weeks to get from North to South on foot.
- Because most of the trail was through neutral countries, the USA and ARVN could not attack troop movements there.

## Now try this

List **two** reasons for the mass bombing campaign. Then give **two** examples of how effective the campaign was.

# Search and destroy

As a response to the increasing threat from the Vietcong, many more US troops came to Vietnam in the 1960s. A new US tactic of 'search and destroy' missions was also developed.

## The problem: increasing Vietcong threat

Following Diem's fall in 1963, the Vietcong got many more recruits and became better organised. Their victory seemed close and tactics developed to cope with US strengths.

- The Vietcong tried to stay close to US troops so that US aeroplanes would not bomb them in case they hit their own side.
- The Vietcong also attacked US air bases to destroy US aircraft. An example is an attack at Bien Hoa in 1964.
- While the Vietcong continued their guerrilla tactics, they also joined with North Vietnamese soldiers in large-scale battles. An example is Binh Gia in 1964.

## US response: troop increases

General Westmoreland was in charge of the US military in Vietnam. He convinced President Johnson that the Vietcong would soon defeat the ARVN unless there was a big increase in US troops.

In 1965, Johnson made the decision to send large numbers of US troops to Vietnam. The number there increased massively: from 23 000 in 1964 to 184 000 in 1965.

This helped the USA to defend South Vietnam, but each year more troops were called for. This increased the number of young men **drafted** (conscripted) into the war, which increased opposition to the war in the USA. The lack of progress also increased opposition.

## US response: search and destroy

The USA set up many fortified bases in South Vietnam. US troops set out from these bases on **search and destroy** missions:

- Small groups would search for Vietcong or their supplies, often hidden in villages.
- US troops would then burn down the village to warn others not to shelter Vietcong. These were called 'Zippo raids', after the Zippo lighters used by US troops.
- When Vietcong fighters were located, troops could call in air strikes and get reinforcements flown in by helicopter.
- Search and destroy aimed to kill as many Vietcong as possible, making it easier for the ARVN to win the civil war. Success was measured in **body count**.
- Search and destroy missions only took place in South Vietnam. Troops were never sent into North Vietnam. The USA did not want to draw China into the war.
- In the first month of search and destroy missions, 1100 Vietcong were killed and only 100 US troops died.

## Search and destroy: impact

Initial success did not continue and there were problems with the US response that had implications for US involvement in Vietnam.

- It was very hard for US troops to tell Vietcong apart from the local population, as they dressed the same as the villagers. This left the US troops constantly on edge and vulnerable to ambushes.
- Burning down villages made local people hate the Americans and increased support for the Vietcong. It also created four million refugees in South Vietnam by the end of the war.
- Once US troops moved out of an area, the Vietcong moved back in. This meant search and destroy missions felt like failures to the US troops even when they achieved high body counts. This had a negative effect on US troop **morale**.
- The Vietcong could break off fights and retreat into countries where the US and ARVN forces could not follow them (North Vietnam, Laos and Cambodia). This made it harder for search and destroy to work.

## Now try this

Identify and explain **three** problems with search and destroy as a way of trying to win the Vietnam War.

# My Lai

The problems and frustrations of search and destroy missions contributed to a massacre of South Vietnamese civilians by US troops in the village of My Lai, in March 1968.

## My Lai Massacre, 1968

On 16 March 1968, US troops were sent to the village of My Lai in South Vietnam, where they were told they would come under Vietcong fire. They found only women, children and old men in the village. They killed everyone they found (at least 347, and possibly over 500, civilians) as well as their animals. After stopping to eat lunch, they returned to base.

Sergeant Ron Haeberle, a war photographer, accompanied the soldiers and took photographs of what happened.

Women and children in My Lai, March 1968, just before US soldiers shot them dead.

## Public impact of the massacre

People in the USA were not sure what to believe about what had taken place. The government was accused of withholding information. Photographs of the massacre were released to CBS News in December and the public saw this as evidence of a serious cover-up. The US public was horrified.

### Trial of Lt Calley, 1970–1971

Lt Calley led the military action at My Lai on the day of the massacre. He claimed that he had been acting on direct orders from his seniors when the massacre was carried out.

The Peers Enquiry later found that Calley was indeed following orders and that high-level army officials, including generals, were involved in the cover-up.

Lt Calley was found guilty of 22 murders and sentenced to life imprisonment – although his sentence was later reduced to three years. Controversially, even though 18 further officers had charges brought against them, no other soldier faced trial.

## My Lai and search and destroy tactics

My Lai shows how search and destroy tactics increased conflict and tension.

- Lt Calley's orders were to clear the area of Vietcong. He was expected to achieve a high body count as evidence of this.
- Charlie Company, the troops involved, had lost many friends to Vietcong snipers without ever seeing the enemy.
- Charlie Company knew women and children could be Vietcong. They were very wary of all Vietnamese people.
- Leaving fortified bases on search and destroy missions was very stressful for US troops because of the risk of ambush.

## Consequences of My Lai

The army covered up My Lai for over a year. Then Sergeant Haeberle's photographs caused worldwide outrage. Coverage of Lt Calley's trial also contributed to increased tensions about US aims, strategies and progress in the war.

- Many Americans were shocked that young US soldiers could kill innocent civilians – even babies. They thought the war had mentally damaged their young men. This increased opposition to the war.
- This reaction meant that US soldiers realised the US public had no idea of what combat in Vietnam was like. This had a negative impact on soldiers' morale.

### Now try this

Describe **two** ways in which the My Lai massacre demonstrates the failure of search and destroy as a tactic. Provide evidence for each point you make.

# The Tet Offensive

The Tet Offensive was a large-scale attack by the North Vietnamese Army (NVA) and Vietcong troops. It shocked the USA because, for months, they had thought the war was nearly over.

## The Tet Offensive: what happened

By 1968, **Le Duan** was in control of North Vietnam. He believed that, if the North launched a major offensive, South Vietnamese people would rise up, overthrow their government and unite with the North.

> 70000 NVA moved into South Vietnam's cities and towns. They smuggled Soviet and Chinese weapons in with them.

⬇

> It was usual for people to travel through Vietnam for the new year (Tet) holiday, so the authorities did not notice.

⬇

> North Vietnam created a diversion: an attack on Khe Sanh, a military base near the border with Laos. US command concentrated their attention there.

⬇

> Early on 30 January 1968, Vietcong and NVA fighters began a series of attacks on more than 100 South Vietnamese towns and cities, including the capital, Saigon.

⬇

> US and ARVN forces were taken by surprise and there was fierce fighting across South Vietnam. The South Vietnamese people hid in their houses and did not join with the communists.

⬇

> 84000 Vietcong and NVA troops took part in the Tet Offensive. 37000 were killed, lost or wounded: perhaps 20% of the communist forces stationed in South Vietnam. The USA lost 2500 soldiers.

## Consequences of the Tet Offensive

The offensive had consequences for the war itself and also for how it was seen in the USA.

The US military took back control of the cities quickly, but they used overwhelming military force. Some cities were left in ruins, for example Hue. Civilians blamed both sides for destroying their lives. No one felt safe.

The Vietcong were very badly damaged by the Tet Offensive. North Vietnam now had to supply fighters for the war in the South. The South Vietnamese people had not risen up and the ARVN had not collapsed – as predicted.

**Consequences for the war**

20 million Americans watched television coverage of the attacks and the brutality used by both sides. This coverage showed the reality of the fighting, increasing anti-war protest.

**Consequences for US public opinion**

In March 1968, another 200000 US troops were to be sent to Vietnam. Johnson's popularity ratings dropped from 40% to 26%. He decided he would not stand for president again when his term ended.

Trusted US newsreader Walter Cronkite told the US public that the USA was not close to victory, as the military and government insisted. Instead, it was stuck in Vietnam with no easy way out.

## Now try this

Complete these **two** sentence starters about the Tet Offensive. Make sure your completed answers include evidence to back up your points.
a) The Tet Offensive was a victory for the USA because…
b) The Tet Offensive was a defeat for the USA because…

# Demands for peace

By 1968, the USA seemed stuck in Vietnam, with no sign of the victory Americans had expected. There were growing demands within the USA for a peaceful solution in Vietnam.

Anti-war movement

The draft system (conscription)

Civil rights issues

Growing student protests

**Demands for peace from within the USA**

Media coverage

For information on media coverage, see page 28.

## The growing anti-war movement

A very small anti-war movement had protested against US involvement in Vietnam since the 1950s. But, in the 1960s, the movement grew much larger and more influential. For example:

- **December 1964:** 25 000 people demonstrated against the war in Washington DC.
- **October 1969:** two million people joined in anti-war demonstrations across the USA.

Some veterans of the Vietnam War formed anti-war groups. One example is Vietnam Veterans Against the War. Their opposition seemed especially powerful and they could not be ignored in the way hippies or communists could be.

## Vietnam and civil rights

In 1967, civil rights leader Martin Luther King declared he was against the war. He argued that spending so much money on the war ($20 billion a year) was wrong when there were so many social problems to fix in the USA.

Another civil rights issue was the draft system. Black Americans often felt they were being sent to Vietnam while white Americans avoided the draft. Boxing celebrity Muhammad Ali was drafted, but refused to go.

Organisations such as Students for a Democratic Society (SDS) coordinated protests to make them more effective. For example, the SDS organised large student demonstrations and made sure the media covered them. This helped the anti-war movement to grow.

## Reasons for growing student protests

- Young people questioned the strict moral code of their parents' generation.
- The hippie movement rejected war and promoted peace and love.
- The civil rights movement attracted a lot of student support, with its emphasis on creating a fairer, more equal USA.
- The draft system conscripted 18–26 year olds. This meant students had friends in Vietnam.

Older Americans were often disgusted by student protests. They accused protestors of wanting the communists to win.

### Impact of protests

Demands to end the war had a major impact on both President Johnson and his successor, President Nixon.

A common protest chant was 'Hey, hey, LBJ, how many kids did you kill today?'. (LBJ was Johnson's nickname.) Constant criticism over failures in Vietnam encouraged Johnson not to run for a second term as president in 1968.

Nixon wanted to escalate bombing campaigns to force North Vietnam to negotiate. But every time he did, massive protests followed. In October 1969, he was forced to delay bombing campaigns because of huge peace protests.

## Now try this

1 The following dates and figures all relate to protests in the USA against the war:
   a) October 1969; b) two million; c) $20 billion; d) 18–26; e) December 1964; f) 25 000.
   Explain each date or figure, identifying the link to protest in each case.
2 Now write a sentence explaining the contrast between the figures 'two million' and '25 000'.

# Vietnamisation

President Nixon worked on several different approaches to get the USA out of Vietnam. However, he still wanted to ensure that South Vietnam did not become a communist-led country.

## The Nixon Doctrine

On 25 July 1969, Nixon put forward his ideas about Vietnam, Southeast Asia and the USA – known as the Nixon Doctrine.

✓ The USA would continue any existing support it had promised its allies and help them against any nuclear attacks.

✓ However, from now on the United States would only provide financial help and training against threats from countries that did not have nuclear capacity – it would not provide soldiers.

In the USA, public opinions differed about Vietnamisation. Some supported the aims of the war and wanted to continue with active involvement. Others wanted American withdrawal as soon as possible.

## Key features of Vietnamisation

Putting the ideas behind the Nixon Doctrine into practice was called **Vietnamisation**. Nixon's strategy was announced on 3 November 1969.

- Nixon wanted US troops to withdraw from Vietnam, while also giving the appearance that the USA had not lost the war.
- The ARVN was to take over more of the fighting, reducing the number of US deaths.
- The US government's focus was now to send money and advisers, not soldiers.
- The US government's aim was to ensure South Vietnam remained an independent, non-communist country – in this way the USA would not lose face over the outcomes.

Vietnamisation failed because US training and equipment was not enough to ensure the ARVN was ready to take over the fighting. The ARVN also suffered from corruption and desertion.

## Impact of Vietnamisation

By the end of 1969, 60000 US troops had left Vietnam.

- Opposition to the war dropped immediately. Opinion polls in November 1969 showed 77% of Americans supported Nixon's approach in Vietnam.
- US soldiers in Vietnam lost motivation to fight. Many tried to avoid conflict situations. Officers who looked for fights were even killed by their platoons.
- The ARVN was strengthened. The USA provided 900000 rifles, 2000 armoured vehicles and 1000 helicopters. The USA paid for the ARVN to recruit one million more soldiers, with a 19% pay rise.
- North Vietnam saw that they were forcing the USA out of the war. Ho Chi Minh told Nixon that North Vietnam was 'determined to fight to the end'.

## Nixon's other strategies

- Bombing campaigns in the North were increased. This aimed to put more pressure on North Vietnam to accept a peace agreement that kept Vietnam divided.
- Nixon also sent officials to peace talks in Paris between North and South Vietnam. However, the delegates could not even agree how to sit around the table.
- In March 1969, Nixon also authorised secret bombing campaigns of parts of the Ho Chi Minh Trail in Cambodia. These had to be secret because the US public would not accept expanding the war in this way.
- In August 1969, Nixon started secret peace talks with North Vietnam. He did not tell his South Vietnamese allies about these. Nor did he let the US public know that he was secretly negotiating with communists.

### Now try this

Describe **one** way in which Vietnamisation reduced conflict in Vietnam. Describe **one** way in which it encouraged an increase in conflict.

# The war widens

One part of Vietnamisation was to build up the ARVN so that it could defend South Vietnam without US troops. Nixon also wanted to weaken the Vietcong and NVA, which meant widening the war. Nixon's aim was to force the North to negotiate and accept the division of Vietnam.

## Widening the war to Cambodia, 1970

- In April 1970, Nixon ordered 50 000 US troops into Cambodia to attack NVA bases after a change of leadership in Cambodia. The new leaders were anti-communist.

- Nixon justified the attacks to the US public by saying the North Vietnamese were helping Cambodia's communists, the **Khmer Rouge**, to take power.

- Widening the war was very unpopular in the USA. There were many protests, including at Kent State University. In 1971, the US Congress banned US troops from being used in Cambodia or Laos again.

- The Khmer Rouge grew rapidly after North Vietnam increased its support. Civil war spread in Cambodia.

- The attacks forced North Vietnam to move bases to Laos. But they did not agree to any US peace demands. Instead they began to build up troops and weapons for a new offensive in 1972.

The bombing campaign of 1970–1972: The end of chemical warfare; Relations with China; Widening the war to Cambodia; Widening the war to Laos

**North Vietnam's Easter Offensive**

### The end of chemical warfare

The USA had used chemicals to kill crops (Agent Blue) and jungle cover (Agent Orange). North Vietnam condemned this as chemical warfare, but the USA denied it. By 1970, it was clear that there were very bad health consequences, such as birth defects. In 1971, Nixon ended their use, against Army wishes. Over 3000 villages had been sprayed – a quarter of South Vietnam – with chemicals 50% stronger than those used in the USA.

For more information on US bombing tactics, see page 20. For more on the Kent State protest, see page 27.

## Widening the war to Laos, 1971

US military planners thought that a massive attack on North Vietnamese bases in Laos could possibly end the war. In February 1971, 17 000 ARVN troops attacked into Laos.

- The ARVN troops had been trained by US advisers, but no US ground troops were allowed to join them in the attack following the US Congress ban.

- The USA was allowed to support the ARVN from the air and with artillery.

- However, the attacks were not a success. NVA reinforcements flooded into the area. Soon the 17 000 ARVN were facing 60 000 NVA troops. The ARVN lost 9000 men and were forced to retreat.

- Vietnamisation had not worked. Nixon's popularity dropped sharply in the USA.

## Relations with China

By 1970, relations between China and the USSR had become very tense. Both wanted to improve their relations with the USA as a consequence. The USA asked China to help pressure North Vietnam into agreeing to peace. However, China continued to send North Vietnam tanks, artillery and missiles.

There was a massive North Vietnam offensive against the South in April 1972, known as the Easter Offensive. The ARVN almost collapsed. In response, Nixon increased US bombing in North Vietnam. Mines were laid in Haiphong harbour, where Chinese ships brought in supplies. Now confident that China would not get drawn directly into the war, Nixon was determined to stop the Easter Offensive.

### Now try this

1 Give **two** reasons to explain why Nixon widened the war with attacks in Cambodia in 1970 and Laos in 1971.
2 Give **two** consequences of Nixon's decision to widen the war.

# Kent State University

Four days after Nixon announced that troops would be sent into Cambodia (April 1970), four American students were shot dead by US National Guards after anti-war protests in Ohio.

## What happened at Kent State, Ohio?

- The student protests at Kent State were part of a wave of demonstrations against the widening of the war into Cambodia.
- The National Guard were called in after violent clashes between protestors and the police alarmed the local town mayor.
- When student protestors threw rocks and shouted abuse at the Guardsmen, some guards panicked and shot around 60 bullets into the crowd, killing four students.

A government report decided that the National Guardsmen had been wrong to shoot. No one was punished, however.

For more information on Cambodia, see page 26.

### Timeline

**Kent State University shootings, 1970**

**2 May** There are several demonstrations and a military training building on campus is set alight.

**4 May** Officials stop a planned demonstration but 2000 people protest anyway. Tear gas does not break up the crowd and they hurl empty canisters and debris at the National Guardsmen. The National Guard open fire.

**1 May** In Ohio, a group of Kent State University students bury a copy of the US Constitution in protest at Nixon's decision to send US troops into Cambodia.

**3 May** The numbers of protestors swell to over 1000 and the mayor declares an emergency. 900 members of the National Guard are called out, armed with rifles and tear gas. Tear gas is used to disperse several demonstrations.

## Consequences of the Kent State shooting

The shooting increased tension over the war:

- Many in the USA were shocked that white middle-class American students had been shot by the National Guard, who were supposed to be protecting US citizens.
- Most Americans were outraged that students had been involved in violent protests – 58% blamed the students for what happened.
- Many students believed the government would kill more students to stop the protests. 400 campuses closed as two million students refused to go to classes.

A month later, two black students were shot and killed, and 12 injured, during protests at the mainly black Jackson State University. There was very little public attention.

## Impact on opposition to the war

- A photograph taken after the shootings by a student photographer, John Filo, shows the dead body of Kent State student Jeffrey Miller. The photograph was used in news reports worldwide. It became a symbol of opposition to the war.
- Five days after the Kent State shootings, there was a demonstration in Washington DC against the war and against the shooting of students. 100 000 people were involved.
- Nixon's first year as president had seen US involvement in Vietnam decrease, which also reduced pressure on the presidency from peace protestors. After the invasion of Laos and Cambodia and the Kent State shootings, however, anti-war protests increased.

### Now try this

Explain **two** ways in which the Kent State shootings increased tension in the USA over the war.

# Media and public opinion

The US military was not allowed to censor (control) media reports about the war. It therefore complained that negative media coverage influenced how the American public viewed the war.

## The media and the military

✓ In 1964 there were only around 20 US news reporters in Vietnam. There was not much public interest in the civil war.

✓ The number of reporters grew rapidly after 1965 because of the decision to send in thousands of US troops. In 1965 there were 400 reporters, 600 by 1968.

✓ Most reporters stayed in Saigon and reported what the military press office told them about the war's progress.

✓ Some went with combat troops on missions and reported what they saw. 60 journalists were killed during the war.

## Turning point in media coverage

Before the Tet Offensive at the start of 1968, most US media coverage supported what the military was doing in Vietnam.

Then, trusted TV newsreader Walter Cronkite reported that the USA looked 'mired in stalemate' and stuck in Vietnam. This contradicted what the US government had said about how the enemy was nearly beaten.

This is seen as a **turning point** in the war: when media coverage became more critical of what the USA was doing in Vietnam. Johnson had lost the confidence of the American public.

For more on Cronkite's statement, see page 23.

## How the media influenced public opinion

• Journalists uncovered stories that the government and military hoped to hide; for example, My Lai and Nixon's secret bombing of Cambodia. These revelations increased mistrust of the government.

• When the media covered stories about the war widening to Cambodia or Laos, large peace demonstrations followed. For example, Nixon's attack on Cambodia was followed by protests at Kent State.

• Photographs of the conflict gave powerful messages about the terrible cost of the war for Americans and Vietnamese alike.

• On 3 November 1969, Nixon appealed on television to the 'silent majority' of Americans to support Vietnamisation. His public support jumped from 55% to 77%. The White House received 30 000 letters and 50 000 telegrams in support.

• Media coverage of anti-war protests encouraged pro-war protests. For example, in May 1970, 'hard hats' (construction workers) were disgusted by students burning US flags. They beat up students protesting about the Kent State shootings.

There is an argument to say that protestors reacted to government action in Vietnam, not to media coverage of it. The biggest cause of public concern was rising US deaths.

## The Watergate scandal

From 1972 until 1974, President Nixon was caught up in allegations that he had ordered secret phone taps on his political rivals. This was called the **Watergate scandal**.

Although Nixon won the 1972 presidential election, the scandal made it harder for him to get decisions approved. Eventually, in August 1974, his guilt was proven by reporters and he was forced to resign. Many Americans now mistrusted their leaders more than ever.

## Impact of Watergate

Without Nixon helping to raise funds to support South Vietnam, the US government was reluctant to pay more money to prevent the South from losing the war.

Nixon's authority was undermined, but the scandal also had an impact on his successor, Gerald Ford. Congress refused further aid, limiting the resources available to Ford's government. When Ford pardoned Nixon, Ford's authority was undermined further.

## Now try this

'Negative media coverage reduced public support for the Vietnam War in the USA.' Outline **two** points that support this argument and **two** points that argue against it.

# The Paris Peace Talks

On 27 January 1973, North Vietnam, South Vietnam and the USA signed an agreement to end the Vietnam War and restore peace. This agreement is known as the Paris Peace Accords.

## Events leading to the Paris Peace Accords

**May–October 1972:** The USA's bombing campaign stops North Vietnam's Easter Offensive from defeating South Vietnam.

**October 1972:** A **breakthrough** in secret negotiations between Kissinger (USA) and Tho (North Vietnam) takes place, with both sides making important concessions. Kissinger tells the US public that the war is about to end.

**November 1972:** Nixon wins a landslide victory to become president for a second term.

South Vietnam's President Thieu, who was not involved in the negotiations, refuses to accept plans for the USA to pull its troops out of South Vietnam without North Vietnam having to do the same.

As a result, North Vietnam backs out of the agreement.

**December 1972:** Nixon orders more bombing campaigns across North Vietnam, with maximum destruction. International criticism compares the actions of the USA to the Nazis.

Nixon promises Thieu that the USA will keep supplying the ARVN and will send its airpower to defend South Vietnam against North Vietnamese attacks. He also threatens to stop the promised billions of dollars in economic development aid if Thieu does not sign the agreement.

**27 January 1973:** The Accords are signed by the three governments and the Vietcong.

## Reasons for the 1972 breakthrough

1. North Vietnam was worried that both China and the USSR were about to stop supporting them. This meant they agreed to allow South Vietnam to be part of peace talks and elections.

2. President Nixon was determined to make progress on peace talks to help him win the 1972 election. This meant the USA agreed to pull its troops out without insisting that North Vietnam also pulled troops out of the South.

3. North Vietnam was badly weakened by the 1972 bombing campaign and losses in the Easter Offensive. It needed time to recover, which a ceasefire would provide.

For more on the Easter Offensive, see page 26.

## Key terms of the Paris agreement

- A ceasefire began as soon as the Accords were signed. Troops from both North and South in South Vietnam were to stay where they currently were.
- All US troops would leave Vietnam.
- US prisoners of war would be released.
- Free elections would be held to decide South Vietnam's future.
- The reunification of Vietnam would be achieved peacefully.
- The USA would replace military equipment needed by South Vietnam to defend itself.

### The role of Kissinger

Henry Kissinger was Nixon's national security adviser. The USA had a whole department of trained diplomats to carry out negotiations, but Kissinger preferred to make deals himself, in secret talks. As well as the Paris Accords, he negotiated better relationships between the USA and China, and the USA and the USSR.

**Now try this**

What was the main reason for the breakthrough in talks in 1972–1973? Write a paragraph to explain your answer.

# The US withdrawal

The Paris Peace Accords ceasefire was quickly broken, and North Vietnamese forces swept south. The USA did not intervene. In April 1975, Saigon fell and Vietnam was unified again.

## Consequences of the Paris agreement

Terms of the Accords:

Events after January 1973:

| Elections | → | President Thieu refused to negotiate with communists or allow any Vietcong into his government. He ordered ARVN attacks to get back territory lost in the Easter Offensive. |

| Ceasefire | → | By March 1973, 6000 ARVN troops had been killed in fights with the Vietcong. The NVA built up its forces in the North but did not attack for fear of US bombing. |

| US support | → | The Watergate scandal undermined Nixon's powerful position. In 1974, Congress refused to send money to Vietnam and prohibited any military operations anywhere in Indochina. |

| US troop withdrawal: completed by March 1973 | → | The economy of South Vietnam collapsed. US troops had spent $400 million a year in South Vietnam. Without them, one in five South Vietnamese people lost their jobs. |

## North Vietnam's victory

- In December 1974, North Vietnam's leadership ordered a test attack to see if the USA would use airpower to defend South Vietnam.

- In three weeks, the NVA easily captured a whole South Vietnamese province. The USA did nothing to help the ARVN.

- President Thieu ordered ARVN troops to retreat. 400000 civilians fled with them. Thousands died from North Vietnamese artillery and from bombs dropped by mistake by ARVN planes.

- By April 1975, the North Vietnamese were attacking Saigon. President Thieu fled the country. The USA scrambled to evacuate all remaining US staff.

- On 30 April 1975, the South surrendered to the North. The war was over. The NVA's attack had taken just 55 days to defeat the ARVN.

## Fall of Saigon, April 1975

Within two months of the Paris agreement, all the remaining US troops in Vietnam were withdrawn, despite North Vietnam breaking the ceasefire during this period.

By April 1975, only around 1000 US citizens were left in Saigon. They were evacuated by helicopter, along with 1100 Vietnamese who had worked for the USA, ending US military and political influence in Vietnam.

The scenes of panic among South Vietnamese trying to escape their own country showed the scale of the USA's failure.

Crowds of Vietnamese and Western people hoping to be evacuated by helicopter from the US embassy in Saigon, 29 April 1975.

When you look at photographs, remember the 5Ws: Who? What? When? Why? Where?

## Now try this

Write a sentence for each of these questions about the photograph above: Who are the people shown? What are they doing? When was it taken? Why are these people here? Where was it taken?

# Reasons for the US defeat

The Americans lacked an understanding of the Vietnamese culture, geographical environment and political landscape, which made it difficult for them to win in Vietnam despite their military strength.

## Lack of knowledge and awareness

**1** Vietnam was very 'alien' to most Americans, who did not understand anything about the country they were fighting in. US soldiers found the war more difficult as a result.

**2** Many Americans underestimated their enemy and held ignorant and racist views about them, considering them an inferior opponent.

**3** US military leaders and strategists did not try to understand the conflict from the viewpoint of the Vietnamese people and this put them at a real disadvantage.

> The geographical distance between the USA and Vietnam is over 13 500 km.

## Political and economic weaknesses

- The USA was fighting a war for which there was no clear public agreement about whether the conflict was justified.

- For the first time in US history, war veterans wanted the war to stop and even handed in their medals in protest.

- There was a lot of media criticism about the war aims and the methods used.

- The US government ignored public opposition to the war but in the end had to listen to the anti-war movement, as presidents and members of Congress relied on public support to be elected.

- When Congress restricted funding of the war after 1971 there were shortages of equipment for US troops.

## Failure of US tactics

The US army benefited from superior military technology, including helicopters and advanced weaponry. However, in Vietnam this did not help the US military to secure a victory. The USA:

- failed in its tactics, mistakenly believing that victory could be won by deploying more troops and ordering more bombing of North Vietnam

- over-estimated its successes, basing calculations on how many villages they destroyed or Vietcong they killed rather than how much territory they controlled.

> US troops were young and inexperienced and lacked relevant training in guerrilla warfare. The failures led to low morale. This in turn led to fragging (the intentional killing of officers by troops) and drug abuse. Many soldiers used alcohol and marijuana. When the US army clamped down on this, soldiers turned to other drugs, including heroin.

## Failure to win hearts and minds

While propaganda claimed the USA wanted democracy for South Vietnam, the South Vietnamese saw the USA as simply a foreign power interfering in their country. So the US-backed South Vietnamese government was very unpopular. It was also hated for its ties to French colonial interests of the past that were seen as anti-Vietnamese.

Many local people in South Vietnam had far more sympathy with the ideas and values of the Vietcong and North Vietnam than with a government imposed on them by the USA.

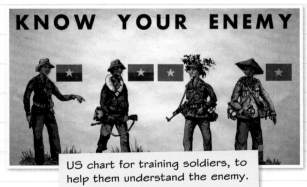

**KNOW YOUR ENEMY**

US chart for training soldiers, to help them understand the enemy.

## Now try this

What do you think was the most important reason why the USA was defeated? Write a short paragraph to explain your answer.

# Vietnam in 1975

In April 1975, Vietnam became a unified communist country, after 30 years of conflict. Saigon was renamed Ho Chi Minh City, in honour of the Northern leader who had died in 1969.

## Strengths of North Vietnam

How had North Vietnam achieved this victory by 1975? Key reasons include:

**1** The North was determined to unite Vietnam and make it independent of foreign control. Everyone knew what they were fighting for: a strong ideology.

**2** Opposing the war in North Vietnam was not an option. Everyone had to contribute, even children. This made it possible for bombing damage to be quickly repaired.

**3** North Vietnam received massive financial and military support from China and, after 1965, from the USSR. This meant North Vietnam had modern weapons and could rebuild its forces after failed offensives, for example after the Tet Offensive.

**4** The Ho Chi Minh Trail allowed North Vietnam to support conflict in South Vietnam. Its routes through neutral Laos and Cambodia were very important because it was difficult for the USA to cut this vital supply route.

**5** North Vietnam's Communist Party leaders did not have to justify their decisions to voters or face criticism from the media, protestors or rival politicians. This meant they could continue to fight despite high numbers of military and civilian deaths.

## Problems of Vietnam in 1975

- In 1975, Vietnam was in ruins. The economy had collapsed. There was a refugee crisis because so many people had fled south to escape the fighting.

- The USA refused to lend any money to a communist country. The USSR provided aid to help develop a Soviet economy. But South Vietnam had been capitalist and the Soviet system failed to work well there.

- In South Vietnam, many people were linked to the government, the ARVN and the USA. Hundreds of thousands tried to escape the country, expecting a massacre.

- The new government did not order a massacre but instead sent 1.5 million people to be 're-educated'. This sometimes meant years in camps, doing forced labour.

- After 1975, farming was taken over by the state. But, in the South, peasants resisted having their land and animals taken away by not working and by killing their livestock. Food supplies collapsed and many people starved.

- After 1975, as the economy continued to suffer, many more Vietnamese left the country as refugees.

## Ho Chi Minh and the North's victory

✓ Ho Chi Minh was a hero. He led the Vietminh to victory against the Japanese and then the French. He declared Vietnam's independence in September 1945.

✓ Ho's role in setting up the Vietcong in the late 1950s was crucial in the civil war.

✓ By 1960, other people had taken over as the leaders of North Vietnam. Ho was a figurehead, used to inspire the people to keep on fighting for a united Vietnam.

This photograph from Saigon in 1975 shows destruction caused by NVA artillery. In 1975, most of Vietnam's cities were in ruins.

## Now try this

State **two** challenges faced by the new government of Vietnam in 1975.

# The price of conflict

The price of conflict in Vietnam was huge. There were many different costs, including social and environmental. Vietnam's people suffered devastating consequences, many of which are still felt in Vietnam today.

**Estimated human cost of the war: Vietnam**
- Soldiers killed: 1.1 million
- Soldiers wounded: 2 million
- Civilians killed: 1.1 million
- Civilians wounded: 5 million
- 42 000 killed by unexploded bombs since the end of the war.

**Human cost of the war: USA**
- Deaths: 58 000
- Wounded: 300 000

**Financial cost of the war: USA**
The USA spent $170 billion (around $1 trillion today) on the war.

**Social and economic costs: Vietnam**
- 7 million tons of US bombs destroyed Vietnam's buildings, roads, bridges, power stations and industries. Vietnam's economy was left in ruins.
- Much of Vietnam's farmland was badly damaged by bombing and defoliants.
- There were 11 million refugees in 1975. 3 million 'boat people' (refugees who fled Vietnam in boats) later escaped Vietnam after the war.

**The cost of the conflict**

**Social cost of the war: USA**
- US society was deeply divided over the Vietnam War for many years.
- Many Vietnam veterans felt rejected when they returned home. No one wanted to talk about the war.
- 15% of Vietnam veterans suffered Post Traumatic Stress Disorder.
- The cost of the war meant social problems in the USA were not fixed, for example poor-quality housing.

**Environmental cost of the war: Vietnam**
- 4 million Vietnamese exposed to Agent Orange.
- 1 million disabled or with health conditions caused by Agent Orange.

**Political cost of the war: USA**
- The USA's international reputation was damaged, especially because it bombed civilians in North Vietnam.
- The USA became more divided politically, and US society became less trusting of its government.

## Vietnamese casualty figures

Neither North or South Vietnam kept accurate casualty figures (people killed or injured). US enemy body counts are also not reliable because the military exaggerated figures (for example, if one platoon killed four and another killed two, the total body count might be reported as 42).

However, it is estimated that:
- ☑ ARVN deaths = 254 000
- ☑ NVA and Vietcong deaths = 850 000
- ☑ South Vietnam civilian deaths = 587 000
- ☑ North Vietnam civilian deaths = 550 000

A photograph from 2014 showing a veteran visiting the Vietnam Veterans Memorial in Washington DC. The memorial lists the names of Americans killed in the conflict in Vietnam.

## Now try this

Look at the diagram above showing the costs of the Vietnam War. Which cost do you feel was most significant and why? Explain your ideas in a short paragraph.

# Exam overview

This page introduces you to the main features and requirements of the Paper 1 Section B exam paper for Conflict and tension in Asia, 1950–1975.

## About Paper 1

- Paper 1 is for your period study and your wider world depth study.

- Section B of the paper will be on your wider world depth study, which is Conflict and tension in Asia, 1950–1975.

- Section B will include questions about other wider world depth study options. You should **only** answer the questions about Conflict and tension in Asia, 1950–1975.

- You will receive two documents: a question paper, which will contain the questions and sources, and an answer booklet.

> The Paper 1 exam lasts for 1 hour 45 minutes (105 minutes). There are 84 marks in total: 40 marks for Section A; **40 marks for Section B**, plus 4 marks for spelling, punctuation and grammar. You should spend about **50 minutes** on Section A and **50 minutes on Section B**, with 5 minutes to check your answers.

> Here we are focusing on Section B and your wider world depth study. However, the same exam paper will also include Section A, where you will answer questions on your period study.

## The questions

> You can see examples of all four questions on pages 38–43, and in the practice questions on pages 44–53.

The questions for Paper 1 section B will always follow this pattern:

**Question 19**
Study **Source K**.
**Source K** … How do you know?
Explain your answer using **Source K** and your contextual knowledge.     **(4 marks)**

> Question 19 targets AO3. AO3 is about analysing, evaluating and using sources to make substantiated judgements. Spend about 6 minutes on this question, which focuses on **analysing a source** and using your own **contextual knowledge**.

**Question 20**
Study **Sources L** and **M**.
How useful are **Sources L** and **M** to a historian studying …?
Explain your answer using **Sources L** and **M** and your contextual knowledge.    **(12 marks)**

> Question 20 also targets AO3. Spend about 14 minutes on this question, which is about **evaluating sources** and using your own **contextual knowledge**.

**Question 21**
Write an account …     **(8 marks)**

> Question 21 targets AO1 and AO2. AO1 is about showing your knowledge and understanding of the key features and characteristics of the topic. AO2 is about explaining and analysing historical events using second order concepts such as causation and consequence. Spend about 10 minutes on this question, which requires you to write a **narrative account**.

**Question 22**
[Statement]
How far do you agree with this statement?
Explain your answer.
    **(16 marks, plus 4 marks for SPaG)**

> Question 22 also targets AO1 and AO2. Spend about 20 minutes on this question, which requires you to make a **judgement** in an **extended response**. Up to 4 marks are available for **spelling, punctuation and grammar** (SPaG).

# Source skills

Questions 19 and 20 are based on **sources**. Question 19 asks you to **analyse one source**, and Question 20 asks you to **evaluate the usefulness of two different sources**.

## What is a source?

A source is something that comes from the time period or event it describes.

A source can be text, such as:

- an account written by someone at the time, such as a letter or diary
- a speech
- a book or government report
- a poem or work of fiction
- a newspaper or magazine article.

It might also be visual, such as:

- a cartoon, photograph, poster or painting
- a plan of a building
- an advertisement
- an object, such as a coin or postcard.

### Contextual knowledge

- ✓ Questions 19 and 20 will both ask you to explain your answer using the sources and your **contextual knowledge**.
- ✓ This means that you need to think about what you know about the event or development and how the sources fit with what you know.
- ✓ Only use knowledge that is **relevant** to the topic in the question and that is linked to what is contained in the source itself.

## Analysing sources

Analysing a source means working out what it's saying. For example, Question 19 asks you to look at a source and use your contextual knowledge to explain how it conveys a particular idea. To do this, think about:

- What is the **intended message** (purpose) of the source?
- What else can we **infer** (work out) from it? Remember, this may not be something the person who created the source intended!
- What can we tell from the **provenance** (origin and nature) of the source?
- Does the information in the source agree with your **contextual knowledge**? What does this tell you?

## Evaluating sources

Question 20 asks you to evaluate 'how useful' two sources are for a particular enquiry – to work out their value or **usefulness**. To evaluate the usefulness of sources, you need to look carefully at the content and provenance of the sources and use your contextual knowledge, too.

**1** **Content**
- What information in the sources is relevant to the enquiry?
- How useful is this information?

 Underline and annotate information in the source to help you with this.

**2** **Provenance**
- Nature: the type of source it is.
- Origins: who produced it and when.
- Purpose: the reason the source was created.
- How do these things impact on the usefulness of the source?

 Remember that this isn't necessarily about the amount of information given. A small piece of information can be very useful!

Remember that an unreliable source can still be useful.

**3** **Context**
- Use your own knowledge of the enquiry topic to evaluate the source.
- Is the information in the source accurate compared with what you know?

 Remember to think about what information is missing from the source as well as what's included.

35

# Source K

This source is referred to in the worked example on page 38.

---

**SECTION B**

**Conflict and tension in Asia, 1950–1975**

**Source K**   A cartoon from a US newspaper, published in 1963, commenting on US relations with South Vietnam. President Kennedy ('JFK') is the shrugging figure. The collapsed Vietnamese statue represents the regime of Ngo Dinh Diem, president of South Vietnam.

You will be given short details on where the source comes from – in this case, the type of source and where and when it was produced.

You will be given some information about the source. In this case, you are told who is represented in the cartoon.

Just Leaned on It a Little . . .

# Sources L and M

These sources are referred to in the worked examples on pages 39 and 40.

**Source L**    A photograph of civilians killed by US troops, taken by Sergeant Ron Haeberle in My Lai on 16 March 1968. Sergeant Haeberle was an army war photographer who took this photograph with his own camera, not his official US Army camera, because he suspected the Army would try to cover it up. The photograph was widely published when the massacre became public knowledge in 1969.

*Annotate the sources with your ideas. If the source is an image, like this one, think about the details you can see and what they might mean.*

**Source M**    From a transcript of the trial of Lieutenant William Calley in September 1969. Lt Calley, a platoon leader in Charlie Company, was accused of murdering 22 civilians at My Lai and leading his men in massacring 200 civilians in total.

> **Question:** All right. Now, what was your intention in connection with the carrying out of [the My Lai] operation as far as any premeditation or intent was concerned?
>
> **Calley:** To go into the area and destroy the enemy that were designated there, and this is it. I went into the area to destroy the enemy, sir.
>
> **Question:** Did you form any impression as to whether or not there were children, women, or men, or what did you see in front of you as you were going on?
>
> **Calley:** I never sat down to analyze it, men, women, and children. They were enemy and just people. ... I was ordered to go in there and destroy the enemy. That was my job on that day. That was the mission I was given. I did not sit down and think in terms of men, women, and children. They were all classified the same, and that was the classification that we dealt with, just as enemy soldiers.

*If the source is a text extract, underline or highlight any important words or phrases and annotate them.*

# Question 19: analysing sources

Question 19 on your exam paper will ask you to explain how you know something about a source, using the source and your own knowledge of the **historical context**. There are 4 marks available for this question.

## Worked example

 **Links** You can revise US intervention under Kennedy on page 18.

Study **Source K** on page 36.

**Source K** is critical of US relations with South Vietnam. How do you know?

Explain your answer using **Source K** and your contextual knowledge.

**(4 marks)**

### Sample answer

President Kennedy is shrugging. This means he did not feel guilty about what happened to the statue. The statue represents the regime in South Vietnam. It is broken because it was not very strong. The message is that the USA caused the regime to collapse, which it shouldn't have done.

### Analysing a source

Analysing a source is working out what it means, including meanings that aren't directly shown.

☑ Think about what is suggested or implied by the source.

☑ Look at the **context** and **provenance** of the source too.

You need to **explain** how the source supports the statement in the question by:

☑ referring to details in the source and linking them to your contextual knowledge.

For more on sources, turn to page 35.

The student identifies a message from the source, but only gives a simple explanation of how this shows that the source was critical.

The student describes the cartoon and identifies some key features. However, they need to give more contextual knowledge to support their points.

## Improved answer

I know the source is critical of US relations with South Vietnam because it shows President Kennedy pretending that he was hardly involved at all in the collapse of Diem's corrupt and fragile regime. The message is that Kennedy was more involved in the collapse of the Diem regime than he claimed. This is shown by his shrug and the caption that makes him seem like a guilty child, saying 'Just Leaned on It a Little...'.

In fact, Kennedy gave support to a military plot to replace Diem, which ended up with Diem and his brother being murdered. The plot was also backed by the CIA. So, the source is actually implying that Kennedy did a lot more than 'just leaning a little' on the Diem regime. It is criticising the US government for being too heavily involved in Vietnam's politics and its civil war. Political cartoons are usually critical, and often aim to highlight mistakes made by their government.

 It is a good idea to **identify the message** of the source clearly from the start, using features from the source to explain how the cartoonist gets their message across.

 Remember to **use details from the source** in your analysis. In this answer the student uses the cartoon's caption 'Just Leaned on It a Little' to support their explanation.

 Make sure you use your **contextual knowledge** to explain the source's message and how that shows it is supportive or critical.

 Make sure you talk about **provenance**. Here the student identifies the purpose of this type of source.

# Question 20: evaluating usefulness 1

Question 20 on your exam paper will ask you to evaluate the usefulness of two sources. There are 12 marks available for this question.

## Worked example

Study **Sources L** and **M** on page 37. How useful are **Sources L** and **M** to a historian studying the public impact of the My Lai massacre (1968)? Explain your answer using **Sources L** and **M** and your contextual knowledge.

**(12 marks)**

 **Links**  Look back at page 22 to revise My Lai.

### Evaluating the usefulness of sources

To judge the usefulness of a source, you need to think about the content of the source, and its provenance.

To evaluate the **content**, look carefully at the source and what it shows. How would it help someone understand the topic mentioned in the question? What details are included? Compare these details with your historical knowledge. Is there anything you would expect to see that isn't there?

To judge the **provenance**, think about what the source is, where it came from and what it was intended for (its purpose).

You have two sources to consider, so evaluate the pros and cons of each. Do the sources complement each other? (This means, does using both together gives you a fuller picture?)

For more on evaluating sources, turn to page 35.

Compare the answer below with an improved version on the next page.

## Sample answer

The photograph in Source L is useful because it was taken at the time of the massacre by someone who was with the soldiers at My Lai – an eyewitness. It is very clear that the victims are not Vietcong fighters because lots of them are babies.

The reason why the photograph was taken is important. The photographer kept it secret because the Army would have probably destroyed this picture to cover up what happened at My Lai. Instead it was used to prove that the massacre had happened.

Source M shows that Calley did not think about women and children as being different from Vietcong. This is useful because it helps explain why the soldiers of Charlie Company could shoot babies. But it doesn't seem very believable because babies couldn't be an enemy to anyone.

The first part of this answer considers the **provenance** of Source L: nature (a photograph) and origin (someone with the soldiers). Make sure you explain why provenance details make the source more or less useful for **both** sources – this is not really done here.

The student begins to **evaluate** Source L by explaining how its purpose (why the photograph was taken) makes this such an important source. Try to make your explanation very clear. This is a little jumbled. Do this for **both** sources.

Now the student looks at Source M's **content** and **how useful** this is for the enquiry. This is a good idea, but the student could have improved it by using more of their own **contextual knowledge** – for example, about the public impact of Lt Calley's trial. Again, **both** sources should be looked at in this way.

# Question 20: evaluating usefulness 2

This page has an improved version of the answer given on page 39.

**Improved answer**

Source L would be very useful for the historian's enquiry. When the photograph was published in 1969, it became very important for anti-war campaigners because it was so shocking. People could not believe that US soldiers would shoot babies. Even supporters of the war began to worry about the effects of this brutal conflict on America's young men.

The photograph was taken by an eyewitness to the massacre, which makes it useful because it is a direct record of something that had just happened. War photographs are not always reliable because, for example, the Army can control which images are published. The Army photographer used his own camera, which meant the Army did not get to censor the image and cover up the massacre. This photograph was used as proof that the massacre took place and that the victims included mothers and babies.

Source M is useful for understanding the public impact of the My Lai massacre because it shows the big difference between what soldiers in Vietnam thought about the war and what the US public thought. In Source M, Calley says that he had been ordered to destroy the enemy in My Lai and that, for him and his men, that meant any Vietnamese people they met: 'I never sat down to analyze it, men, women, and children. They were enemy and just people.' This was not acceptable to the US public, who had assumed that US soldiers were the good guys, fighting evil Vietcong communists. Instead US soldiers looked worse than the communists.

Source M is a reliable account of the trial because what Calley said would have been recorded by an official person and lots of people would have been present to confirm what he said, and what questions he was asked. This makes it useful to historians. However, Calley may not have been telling the truth. It is very difficult to look at the scene captured in Source L and imagine that Calley and his men saw these babies as a threat. Source M is only an extract from the transcript of a longer trial, though, which also limits its usefulness. More reasons for the massacre may come out later in the transcript.

Remember that the question is asking 'how useful' for a **specific** enquiry – the public impact of My Lai in this case. This answer starts well as it uses impressive **contextual knowledge** to explain why the content of this image had such a significant impact on public opinion.

This is a clearer explanation of why the origin, nature and purpose of the source make it useful. Make sure that you **link provenance back to 'how useful'** for the enquiry. It is easy to say 'it is useful because it is an eyewitness account', without explaining **why** that makes it useful.

Consider the **limitations** of the sources as well as their strengths. For example, the student says here that official war photographs are not always reliable because they were censored by the Army.

Notice how the student has kept their focus on **how useful** the sources are for understanding the public impact of the My Lai massacre.

Here the student has used a powerful quotation from Source M. This adds detail to the answer, which is a good way of supporting and developing the explanation.

Focus on **evaluating** and **making judgements** about the **usefulness** of the sources, not just describing them. Here the student considers how the nature and purpose of the source add to utility. But they also consider how the origin makes Source M less useful without other sources to support it.

# Question 21: narrative account

Question 21 on your exam paper requires you to write a narrative account analysing how and why a historical event happened. There are 8 marks available for this question.

## Worked example

Write an account of how events following the Inchon landings led to increased international tensions in 1951.

**(8 marks)**

🔗 **Links** You can revise the Inchon landings and their consequences on pages 7–10.

Your account will analyse how an event is linked to international consequences: how it became a **wider** issue.

### What is a narrative account?

A **narrative account** is not simply a description of what happened. To write a successful narrative account, you need to:

- ✓ think about **key elements** of the event and how they were **connected**
- ✓ consider what you have been asked to do – you may need to think about **cause** and/or **consequence** here
- ✓ use your **own knowledge** of the period
- ✓ structure your narrative logically, so it clearly explains the **sequence** of events.

## Sample answer

Before MacArthur captured the port of Inchon in September 1950, South Korea had nearly been defeated by North Korea. As a result of the successful landings, the UN forces were able to recapture Seoul. North Korean soldiers in the South were quickly defeated as they became trapped between the new forces to the north and the South Korean forces breaking out from the south.

At that point the UN could have decided that their job was done: South Korea had been defended. But, instead, UN forces advanced into North Korea in October 1950. This was because the UN now wanted to reunify Korea and defeat communism. However, the actual consequence was very different. China felt threatened by the UN's advance. As a result, China joined the war, adding 300 000 troops to North Korea's army.

This was the most significant reason why conflict and tension increased in Korea. It meant the UN forces were pushed back, and the two sides became locked in a stalemate by 1951. MacArthur argued that China would not join the war, but was proved wrong. Also, the USSR secretly aided China and the North Koreans. This could easily have led to nuclear war between the USA and the USSR.

So, by 1951, the situation was very tense. Instead of the consequence of a reunited Korea, which both the UN and North Korea had aimed for, Korea remained divided, with the world's superpowers heavily involved on both sides.

 Start with a **clear introduction** that focuses your analysis on what changed as a result of the event or events in the question. This student has done that by considering the situation before the Inchon landings.

 Use your **own knowledge** of the period. Here, the information about the UN victory shows use of relevant knowledge.

 Use phrases such as 'as a result' or 'this meant that' to create a clear account and show you are considering **consequences**. This helps to make good links between events.

 To make your answer stronger, identify which part of your account you consider to be the most important in leading to the international consequence. Remember to **explain why** it is the most important!

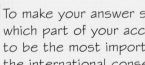 Explain clearly how the events led to the consequence. Don't simply recount the key events one after the other, but **explain how** they led to increased international tensions by 1951.

# Question 22: extended response 1

Question 22 on your exam paper will ask you to write an **extended response** showing a sustained line of reasoning and making a judgement. You will be given a statement and asked **how far** you agree with it. There are 16 marks available for this question, plus 4 marks for spelling, punctuation, grammar and use of historical terminology.

## Worked example

'The main reason why the USA lost in Vietnam was opposition to the war in the USA.'
How far do you agree with this statement? Explain your answer.

**(16 marks, plus 4 marks for SPaG)**

 **Links**   You can revise reasons why the USA lost the Vietnam War on page 31.

Write a list of points **for** and **against** the statement in the question before you start writing your answer.

### 'How far...' questions

This question asks you to weigh **evidence** to come up with an argument – a **line of reasoning**. You need to:

✓ consider evidence that supports the statement in the question, explaining why it **supports** the statement

✓ do the same for any evidence that **contradicts** the statement

✓ develop a **sustained** line of reasoning – 'sustained' means you need to present a clear, logical argument **throughout your answer**

✓ make a **judgement** – you need to decide 'how far' you agree and then back that up with evidence from your answer.

## Sample answer

I don't agree with the statement that the main reason the USA lost was opposition to the war. There was opposition to the war but there were always more people in the USA who supported the war.

Instead I think the reason the USA lost the war was because of Vietcong guerrilla tactics. One tactic was tunnels. That meant the Vietcong could take shelter from US artillery. Other tactics were sabotage and spying. Another tactic was ambushes.

The Ho Chi Minh Trail was another factor that was important. It was a network of paths cleared in the jungle that led from North Vietnam to different parts of South Vietnam. Most of it was not in Vietnam, but went through Laos and Cambodia, where US forces could not go because they were other countries.

In conclusion, I do not agree with the statement because opposition was usually not that strong in the USA compared to support for the war and because actually it was the Vietcong guerrilla tactics that were the main reason.

 **Links**   You can revise Vietcong tactics on page 16.

Compare this answer with an improved version on the next page.

Start your answer with a clear statement, signposting your argument.

All your points should be supported with **evidence**. Here, the student gives basic evidence but this could be expanded with accurate facts and figures. Make sure you fully examine both sides of the argument.

The student has identified a different main reason for the USA losing the war. The reason is appropriate, but although the student gives examples, they don't explain why these tactics meant the USA lost. Try to keep your **focus** on explaining why.

This information is correct, but the student hasn't used it to explain why the USA lost in Vietnam.

You need a **conclusion** that gives your **judgement** about how far you agree, and backs it up. This conclusion fails to back up the judgement and explain **why** Vietcong tactics were so important.

# Question 22: extended response 2

This page has an improved version of the answer on page 42.

**Improved answer**

In my opinion other reasons were more important than opposition to the war. The determination of the North Vietnamese and the lack of support in the South were also vital.

Opposition to the war did increase after events like the Tet Offensive in 1968 or the discovery of the My Lai massacre in 1969 were revealed by the media. For example, in October 1969, two million people demonstrated across the USA against the war. However, opinion polls showed that 77% of Americans in November 1969 actually supported the war: a clear majority. This meant the government could ignore opposition and continue the war.

On the other hand, a lot of the opposition to the war came because the US troops seemed unable to make progress against the Vietcong. Faced by guerrilla tactics such as sabotage, ambushes and bombings, US troops lost motivation to win the war. Because their enemy could hide among ordinary people, US troops were always suspicious of South Vietnamese people, and burnt villages and killed civilians in search and destroy missions. This meant that the South Vietnamese did not support the US soldiers or the ARVN, which made it very difficult for the USA to win the war.

By the end of the war, 1.1 million Vietnamese soldiers had been killed and 1.1 million civilians. After the Tet Offensive, the Vietcong was almost wiped out as a fighting force. The USA lost far fewer men in the 15 years of the war – 58 000. This showed that US tactics were ultimately effective in achieving their aim – to kill the enemy. But, all the same, the USA lost the war. This convinces me that the main reason was actually the commitment of North Vietnam to liberating all Vietnam from foreign control. This commitment meant that, whatever the USA did – for example, the incredible devastation of Operation Rolling Thunder – Vietnamese people would continue to fight them, at any cost.

In conclusion, most Americans supported the war rather than opposed it, so opposition was not the main reason for the USA's defeat. Although US troops faced major difficulties in making progress against Vietcong tactics, they did succeed in killing huge numbers of enemy soldiers. This would have meant a US victory in a normal war, but the North Vietnamese were fighting a guerrilla war. Therefore, my view is that the main reason for the US defeat was the determination of the Vietnamese.

Remember that, for this question, four additional marks are available for good **spelling, grammar, punctuation** and use of historical **terminology**.

This introduction clearly signposts whether the student agrees or not, and gives other reasons for the USA losing the war.

Highlighting key points raised in the statement will help you focus on the arguments that you need to **evaluate** to make your judgement.

Using phrases like 'however', 'on the other hand' or 'but, all the same' clearly demonstrates that you are moving on to another part of your argument, and shows that your answer is following a clear **structure** and has a **sustained line of reasoning**.

Considering more than one reason will help to make your answer stronger. Here the student looks at several reasons: Vietcong tactics, problems with US tactics and the impact on support for the USA in South Vietnam. The student explains how these contributed to the USA losing the war.

Use relevant **facts and figures** to back up your points. Notice how this student has used figures to support their argument about which reasons were most important. Use **specific historic vocabulary** as well: 'Vietcong', 'tactics', 'Tet'.

Here the student identifies which reason they think is the main reason. Notice how the answer has weighed up different options and then made a **judgement** as to why it was most important, and why.

Finish with a clear **conclusion**, stating clearly 'how far' you agree with the statement: your **judgement**. You need to back up your judgement – do this by summarising the arguments in the rest of the answer rather than by introducing new information.

# Practice

You will need to refer to the source below in your answer to question 19 on page 46.

**SECTION B**

**Conflict and tension in Asia, 1950–1975**

**Source K**    A leaflet distributed in North Korea during the Korean War, 1950–1953, by US-led United Nations forces. The leaflet shows a thin, shabbily dressed mother with her starving child. The well-fed person on the right is Kim Il-Sung.

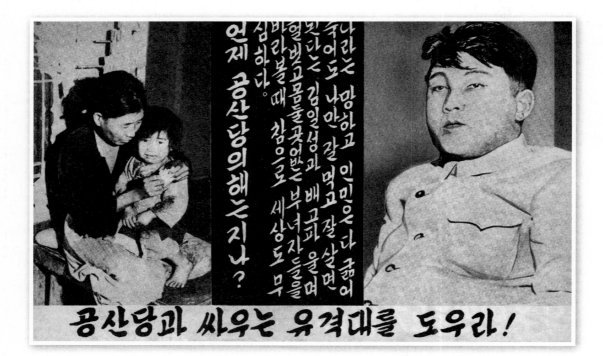

# Practice

You will need to refer to the sources below in your answer to question 20 on page 47.

**Source L**   A photograph showing a strategic hamlet in South Vietnam, including several lines of defensive barricades, in the 1960s.

**Source M**   An extract from an official report by Robert McNamara, the US Secretary of Defense, about his visit to Vietnam in May 1962. The report was classified as top secret.

> The Strategic hamlet program undertaken near Ca Mao on the Delta presented an equally impressive picture… Here, the commander of the 31st Infantry Regiment had gone into an area 95% controlled by the VC, declared martial law, and resettled 11,000 people (some under duress[1]) in 9 strategic hamlets, while fighting the VC wherever he found them… Since [the start] of the program, none of his villages have been attacked, and the freedom from VC taxation (extortion) is proving most appealing to the people. It is the commander's hope (doubtless optimistic) that he will be able to turn the whole area over to the Civil Guard and Self Defense Corps within 6 months.

[1]**under duress**: by force

# Practice

Put your skills and knowledge into practice with the following question. You will need to refer to Source K on page 44 in your answer.

---

**19** Study **Source K**.

**Source K** is critical of the North Korean leadership in the Korean War. How do you know?

Explain your answer using **Source K** and your contextual knowledge.

**(4 marks)**

**Guided** This leaflet is very critical of the North Korean

leadership because it implies that Kim Il-Sung

............................................................................

............................................................................

............................................................................

............................................................................

............................................................................

............................................................................

............................................................................

............................................................................

............................................................................

............................................................................

............................................................................

............................................................................

............................................................................

............................................................................

............................................................................

............................................................................

---

You have 1 hour 45 minutes for the **whole** of Paper 1, which means you have 50 minutes for Section B. You should use the time carefully to answer all the questions fully. In the exam, remember to leave 5 minutes to check your work when you've finished both Sections A and B.

Spend around 6 minutes on this answer. You need to **identify features** in the source and use your **own knowledge**.

**Links** You can revise Kim Il-Sung's leadership on page 4.

You can revise how to analyse sources on page 35.

Remember to **make inferences** from the source to show you are analysing it. Infer means working out something that isn't shown directly. An example of a suitable inference might be that Kim Il-Sung has been neglecting his people instead of helping them.

Make a claim based on evidence from the source about the intended **purpose** of the source: what **message** is the USA giving the North Korean people by showing them as hungry and miserable, in contrast to the North Korean leadership? How does the origin of the source (who produced it) affect its message?

Link your argument to your **own contextual knowledge** of the period. For example, why did a communist leader in North Korea worry the USA?

Make sure you give **examples** from the source to back up what you say.

# Practice

Put your skills and knowledge into practice with the following question. You will need to refer to Sources L and M on page 45 in your answer.

**20** Study **Sources L** and **M**.

How useful are **Sources L** and **M** to a historian studying the effectiveness of the Strategic Hamlets programme?

Explain your answer, using **Sources L** and **M** and your contextual knowledge.

**(12 marks)**

**Guided** Source L is an aerial photograph of a strategic hamlet in the 1960s. This is useful because

.................................................................

.................................................................

.................................................................

.................................................................

.................................................................

.................................................................

.................................................................

.................................................................

.................................................................

.................................................................

.................................................................

.................................................................

.................................................................

.................................................................

.................................................................

.................................................................

.................................................................

.................................................................

.................................................................

.................................................................

.................................................................

.................................................................

.................................................................

You should spend about 14 minutes on this answer.

You have to **evaluate** what is useful about the sources. That means thinking about ways in which each source might be useful for the question and also ways they might be less useful.

**Links** You can revise the Strategic Hamlets programme on page 18.

You can revise how to **evaluate** sources on page 35.

Remember, there are different ways to **evaluate** 'how useful' the sources are: their **content** (what they say), their **provenance** (nature, origin), their **purpose** and by comparing them with your **own contextual knowledge**.

Make sure you relate strengths and weaknesses of the sources to the question: in this case, how useful are the sources for understanding how effective the strategic hamlets were?

It is a good idea to jot ideas around the sources as you are thinking about what to write. You are allowed to do this in the exam, although these notes won't count towards your mark.

# Practice

Use this page to continue your answer to question 20.

..................................................
..................................................
..................................................
..................................................
..................................................
..................................................
..................................................
..................................................
..................................................
..................................................
..................................................
..................................................
..................................................
..................................................
..................................................
..................................................
..................................................
..................................................
..................................................
..................................................
..................................................
..................................................
..................................................
..................................................
..................................................
..................................................
..................................................

You can consider each source independently. You can also consider how the sources are useful when considered together.

Considering **provenance** can often be useful for identifying weaknesses or limitations. Are there ways in which the author or creator of the source was biased? Were they in a situation that meant they only had a limited understanding of the whole situation?

Just because a source is **unreliable** doesn't necessarily mean it is not **useful**. For example, propaganda will not give a reliable account of the situation, but it is useful for showing what a regime or government wanted people to believe.

Remember, you need to identify and **evaluate** the strengths and weaknesses of **both** sources and make a judgement.

# Practice

Put your skills and knowledge into practice with the following question.

**21** Write an account of how events in the Gulf of Tonkin increased the international crisis in Vietnam in 1965.

**(8 marks)**

**Guided**   The Gulf of Tonkin incident in August 1964 was

when a US warship, the *USS Maddox*,

...................................................................

...................................................................

...................................................................

...................................................................

...................................................................

...................................................................

...................................................................

...................................................................

...................................................................

...................................................................

...................................................................

...................................................................

...................................................................

...................................................................

...................................................................

...................................................................

...................................................................

...................................................................

...................................................................

...................................................................

You should spend about 10 minutes on this question.

'Write an account' means you have to give a narrative that **explains the connections**. Don't just describe what happened.

**Links** You can revise the Gulf of Tonkin incident on page 19.

Keep your answer focused on the question. You might remember lots of detail about events in the Gulf of Tonkin in 1965, but you need to focus on the **consequences** these events had on the international crisis.

Make sure you use your **own knowledge** of the period, by describing how factors combined to bring about an outcome – in this case, how different factors came together to result in the USA rapidly escalating its involvement in the Vietnam War.

10 minutes is not very long so remember to **keep your account focused**: resist the temptation to write down everything you can remember about the topic in the question.

# Practice

Use this page to continue your answer to question 21.

..........................................................................

..........................................................................

..........................................................................

..........................................................................

..........................................................................

..........................................................................

..........................................................................

..........................................................................

..........................................................................

..........................................................................

..........................................................................

..........................................................................

..........................................................................

..........................................................................

Question 21 has a focus on how tension and conflict increased from the first event to the international crisis at the end. It is a good idea to identify points at which tension increased and explain them.

You may be able to identify some events that were more important than others in leading to or causing the increased international crisis. This will make your analysis stronger.

To make sure you **analyse the links** between factors, try to use phrases such as: 'because', 'this led to', 'as a result', 'resulted in'. This will help you make sure that your answer follows a **logical structure**.

# Practice

Put your skills and knowledge into practice with the following question.

**22** 'The main reason for the Korean War, 1950–1953, was the division of Korea in 1945.'

How far do you agree with this statement?

Explain your answer.

**(16 marks, plus 4 marks for SPaG)**

**Guided**  Many factors were important in causing the Korean

War, and the division of Korea in 1945 was certainly one of

the most important. In my opinion,

...................................................................................

...................................................................................

...................................................................................

...................................................................................

...................................................................................

...................................................................................

...................................................................................

...................................................................................

...................................................................................

...................................................................................

...................................................................................

...................................................................................

...................................................................................

...................................................................................

...................................................................................

...................................................................................

...................................................................................

...................................................................................

You should spend about 20 minutes on this question.

Remember, this question demands an **extended response** and you will also receive marks for your **spelling, punctuation and grammar**. Write and check your work carefully!

Quickly **plan** your answer before you start writing. List points that support the statement in the question and list other points that go against the statement.

Start with an **introduction** that clearly signposts whether you agree or not, and gives other reasons you will consider.

🔗 **Links** You can revise causes of the Korean War on pages 1–6.

Make sure your answer stays focused on the question you have been asked and **keep your answer relevant throughout**. Don't just write everything you know about the topic.

This is a 'how far' question so you need to **weigh up evidence**: points that support the statement and points that argue against it. Considering more than one reason will help make your answer stronger.

# Practice

Use this page to continue your answer to question 22.

..................................................................
..................................................................
..................................................................
..................................................................
..................................................................
..................................................................
..................................................................
..................................................................
..................................................................
..................................................................
..................................................................
..................................................................
..................................................................
..................................................................
..................................................................
..................................................................
..................................................................
..................................................................
..................................................................
..................................................................
..................................................................
..................................................................
..................................................................
..................................................................
..................................................................
..................................................................
..................................................................
..................................................................
..................................................................
..................................................................

It is a good idea to **signpost** your answer by beginning each paragraph with a clear statement to give the reader an idea of how the answer will develop. For example, 'The division of Korea was a main reason because…' and 'However, this only happened because…'
This will make it easier to write and will make your answer easier to understand. It will also show that you are developing **a clear line of reasoning** and show that you are considering **evidence** from both sides.

Remember, you need to explain causes for this question.
Keep your focus on **explaining why**. A good way to signpost explanations is to use phrases like 'this was because' or 'this caused' or 'the reason for this was'.

Back up your points by using your own **contextual knowledge** and understanding, for example relevant **facts and figures**. A good model to follow is PEE: point, evidence, explain – make a point, back it up with evidence, explain why it was a reason.

# Practice

Use this page to continue your answer to question 22.

...................................................................

...................................................................

...................................................................

...................................................................

...................................................................

...................................................................

...................................................................

...................................................................

...................................................................

...................................................................

...................................................................

...................................................................

...................................................................

...................................................................

...................................................................

...................................................................

...................................................................

...................................................................

...................................................................

...................................................................

...................................................................

...................................................................

...................................................................

...................................................................

End your answer with a conclusion, giving a clear **judgement** about **how far** you agree with the statement in the question.
Your conclusion should start by stating whether you agree or not (or how far you agree, for example, 'I mostly agree... but...'). Then briefly summarise the main points from your answer to back up your judgement.

Try to leave a little time to **check your answer** once you've finished. Look out for any spelling mistakes or punctuation errors. A common mistake is to forget to use a capital letter to start a sentence, or to finish a sentence with a full stop. Make sure you use specific historical vocabulary as well.

# ANSWERS

*Where an exemplar answer is given, this is not necessarily the only correct response. In most cases there is a range of responses that can gain full marks.*

## SUBJECT CONTENT
### Conflict in Korea

### 1. Causes of the conflict

1  The four main causes in the diagram are:
   - the impact of the Second World War
   - nationalism and civil war
   - the impact of the Cold War (1945–1991)
   - US relations with China.
2  The impact of the Second World War.

### 2. The Cold War

One from the following:
- Truman thought communism should be contained because communism threatened people's freedom to choose their own government.
- The USA wanted to encourage capitalism and free trade – it needed to have capitalist countries to buy US products and for the USA to trade with.
- Truman did not want communism to spread to the USA. US fears of communism were later exploited by Senator McCarthy against US officials.

### 3. US relations with China and Korea

1  For example, any two from:
   - US government officials thought that they had 'lost' China to communism because they hadn't done enough to support the opposition to the Communist Party in China's civil war. (China's huge population made it an important country.)
   - In the USA, Senator McCarthy had begun a campaign against American communists who might be trying to make the USA a communist country, and who could be weakening the USA, for example by spying for the USSR.
   - In Europe, the USSR had made sure that Eastern European countries, such as Hungary and East Germany, were controlled by communist parties. The USSR had promised in international agreements to allow these countries to choose their own government, but the USA could see that they'd been wrong to trust the USSR about this.
2  For example, one from:
   - Accepting Koreans to fight with Chinese forces against the Japanese.
   - Allowing Koreans in China to set up a Korean government-in-exile.

### 4. The division of Korea

For example, two from:
- Both leaders of the two halves of Korea wanted Korea to be united, but the leaders of the North wanted a communist Korea and the leaders of the South wanted a capitalist Korea. Both asked for aid to overthrow the other.
- The division of Korea created a communist North and an anti-communist/a capitalist South. The clash between these two political systems created tension that led to conflict.
- The Cold War was responsible for the division of Korea as the USA tried to prevent the USSR occupying all of Korea. The USSR then backed North Korea and the USA South Korea, creating tension that led to conflict.

### 5. Invasion by the North

For example, to support the statement, two from:
- The war began when North Korea invaded. If Kim Il-Sung had not ordered the invasion, there would not have been a war.
- Kim wanted to invade South Korea in order to reunite Korea as a country. This tension led to the invasion, which was the main cause of the war.
- Kim saw the attacks on South Korean communists by Rhee's government. He was sure that the South Korean people would rise up against Rhee to support communism in a united Korea and to support Kim's land reforms.

For example, against the statement, two from:
- The invasion only took place once Stalin had given his permission. Therefore, the main reason for the war was Stalin's control over communist leaders in North Korea and in China.
- The main reason was the division of Korea. If Korea had not been divided, then the tensions between north and south would not have existed. As a result, North Korea and South Korea wouldn't have existed either, so no invasion would have taken place.
- The main reason was tension between the USA and the USSR – the Cold War. Korea was divided because the USA wanted to prevent the USSR from taking control over the whole of Korea, and the USSR held off giving support to the invasion of South Korea until they also had atomic bombs and the USA was distracted with Japan.

### 6. Responses to invasion

The USSR refused to take part in the UN because the USA would not allow communist China to join the UN Security Council. This meant that the USSR was absent from the Security Council meeting in June 1950. The consequence of this was that the USSR could not use its veto to block the USA's proposal to send UN military forces to defend South Korea from attack.

### 7. The UN campaign in the South and North

For example, to support the statement, two from:
- Before the Inchon landings, North Korean forces were in control of almost all of Korea and the UN and South Korean forces were trapped in the southern tip of Korea, around Pusan. It was the success of the Inchon landings that allowed South Korea to be recaptured.
- The success of the Inchon landings meant that the USA changed its objectives from containing communism (defending South Korea) to pushing communism back (advancing into North Korea), which pulled China into the war.
- The Inchon landings were an outstanding achievement by MacArthur because it was technically so difficult to achieve this amphibious assault. The landings demonstrated the military expertise of the USA.

For example, against the statement, two from:
- The main event of the Korean War was the Chinese response to UN forces invading North Korea, because their massive attack pushed the UN forces back deep into South Korea and completely changed the nature of the war: it became a stalemate, a war of attrition.
- The main event of the Korean War was the North's invasion of South Korea in June 1950, because this was the event that started the war in the first place, and the event that brought the USA and UN into the conflict.
- The main event was the USA's decision to use military force to defend South Korea. The UN would probably not have sent troops into Korea without the USA's persuasion. If the USA had not intervened, South Korea would probably have been defeated in September or October 1950, and Korea would have been reunited under a communist government.

- The main event was the defence of Pusan during August and September 1950. The North Koreans were worn down by their attempts to capture Pusan. This meant that, by the time the UN attacked to recapture South Korea, the North's troops were already exhausted and short of supplies.

## 8. Advance into North Korea

The extract does give a clear message by its use of the word 'repel': the UN's aim was to push the North Korean forces back to North Korea, but no more than that. However, it is not completely clear: '…such assistance as may be necessary' is vague. It also says that the aim is to 'restore international peace and security in the area': this is also vague. The 'area' could be South Korea or all of Korea. The aim could include attacking North Korea in order to prevent further attacks on South Korea, or even to reunify Korea and restore peace and security that way.

## 9. China's reaction

1  For example, any two from:
   - It shows that the Chinese forces worked together with the North Korean forces, which would have made them more effective in defeating the UN forces – for example, the North Koreans would have known how best to get from place to place.
   - It shows that the Chinese troops were well equipped because they are carrying modern Soviet-supplied submachine guns.
   - It shows the difficult mountain terrain that was very hard for the UN troops to fight in because they could get trapped in narrow valleys and cut off from reinforcements. The Chinese and North Korean troops are wearing warm padded uniforms and fur hats, which suggests they are prepared for the difficult mountain conditions.
2  It is criticising MacArthur for trying to widen the USA's war in Korea into an attack on communist China, which the cartoonist suggests would then risk causing World War III. It shows this with MacArthur levering a hat – the USA – over a cliff edge labelled 'World War III in Asia'. The risk is that attacking communist China would cause the USSR to respond, because the USSR and China were allies. The caption of the cartoon is 'Not a general's job', criticising MacArthur for making political decisions – widening the war to attack China – instead of doing his job, which was to follow the orders of President Truman.

## 10. Stalemate and peace talks

Your answer is likely to include the following key points and should make links between them:
- The division of Korea in 1945 created tensions between North and South.
- Once the USSR had given its permission, communist North Korea launched its invasion on 25 June 1950. However, this led to a strong reaction by the USA, which was determined to prevent communism spreading to South Korea.
- As a result, the USA persuaded the UN to send a military force to defend South Korea. By September 1950, the UN's forces were successful in defeating the North's attack in the South.
- Because of this success, the USA saw the opportunity to roll back communism. The UN troops advanced into North Korea.
- This caused China to enter the war because it was worried that the USA aimed to attack China too, which had become a communist country in 1949.
- In November 1950, 300 000 Chinese troops defeated the UN troops in North Korea. The UN retreated into South Korea. After several more attacks and retreats, by spring 1951, the two sides faced each other along the 38th parallel. Attempts to agree a peace treaty failed and conflict escalated, increasing the international crisis.

## 11. Korean War: impact

For example, to support the statement, any two from:
- Korea suffered the highest casualties in the war, with over two million deaths estimated, the majority being civilians. Such high casualty figures were a disaster because of the impact on families and on the economy.

- Korea had been divided by the superpowers and the war just continued this division. This has been a disaster for Korea because its people are separated, with families remaining divided, and its potential has been limited.
- Both North Korea and South Korea were devastated by the war. By the end of the war, US bomber pilots often reported that there was nothing left to bomb. The USA dropped more bombs on North Korea (635 000 tons) than it had used in all its campaigns in the Pacific in the Second World War, not including atomic bombs. The level of total devastation was a disaster.

For example, to argue against the statement, any two from:
- Although the Korean War involved huge suffering, it did result in South Korea being defended from takeover by a communist regime. It also resulted in North Korea being defended from takeover by a corrupt and restrictive government led by Syngman Rhee.
- After the Korean War, South Korea received massive US support to aid its recovery. This eventually resulted in it becoming a very successful, economically powerful country. North Korea rebuilt quickly due to Soviet aid.
- The Korean War started as a civil war between nationalists who were both determined to reunite their country. The disaster for Korea was that it was divided in the first place, as a result of superpower tensions.

## Escalation of conflict in Vietnam

## 12. End of French rule

The main reason was that the USA was worried that, if Vietnam became communist, then other countries in the region would probably quickly become communist too, for example Cambodia and Laos. Because the USA did not want the communist Vietminh to rule Vietnam, it became involved to help France in its fight against the Vietminh.

## 13. Dien Bien Phu

a)  Your reasons for the French defeat should include:
   - superior Vietminh tactics
   - over-confident French tactics
   - support from the local population
   - support from China.
b)  Your consequences should include:
   - French surrender
   - French decision to leave Vietnam
   - the Geneva Agreement
   - popularity for Ho Chi Minh and Giap.

## 14. Civil war in South Vietnam

a)  The ARVN was the Army of the Republic of Vietnam and was created by Diem to defend his Republic of Vietnam (South Vietnam).
b)  The NLF was the National Liberation Front, set up by Ho Chi Minh and the North Vietnamese leadership to fight for communism in South Vietnam.
c)  Ho Chi Minh was leader of the North Vietnamese government.
d)  The Republic of Vietnam was the official name for the country of South Vietnam.
e)  Ngo Dinh Diem was the US-backed leader of South Vietnam.
f)  Bo Dai had been the previous leader of South Vietnam, appointed by the French, and was Diem's rival in the referendum for the leadership of South Vietnam.

## 15. Opposition to Diem

Answers will depend on your own reconstruction of the spider diagram on page 15. The five main reasons in the diagram are:
- persecution of communists
- resettlement of peasants
- nepotism
- corruption
- persecution of Buddhists.

## 16. The Vietcong

Any two from:

- Guerrilla tactics meant ARVN troops were ambushed, which meant they had no warning of the attack.
- It was difficult for the ARVN to tell who Vietcong fighters were because they blended in with the local population.
- The Vietcong were very good at getting information about ARVN weaknesses from spying and using the local population to gather information, which meant they knew when to attack and when to hide.

## 17. The Domino Theory

The Domino Theory said that, if Vietnam became communist – in other words if North and South Vietnam became a single communist country – then other countries in the region would quickly follow, for example Vietnam's neighbours Laos and Cambodia. The USA had a policy of trying to contain the spread of communism, and so became involved in South Vietnam. They aimed to stop it becoming communist, both by helping the South Vietnamese fight their civil war against the Vietcong and by helping the government develop the Republic as a successful and strong capitalist country.

## 18. Eisenhower and Kennedy

For example, any two from:

- The number of military advisers increased significantly. Under Eisenhower there were around 700 military advisers working alongside the ARVN and helping to train them. By 1963 this had risen to 16,000 military advisers.
- Under Kennedy's presidency, US military advisers became directly involved in setting up strategic hamlets to protect peasant villages from Vietcong propaganda and attacks. US advisers encouraged the ARVN to work with peasants to try to win their hearts and minds.
- In 1961, Kennedy sent US pilots and helicopters to Vietnam to transport ARVN troops. This had not happened before. Having helicopter transport made it possible for ARVN troops to react to information about Vietcong troop movements much more quickly and hunt down Vietcong cells.

## 19. The Gulf of Tonkin incident

To support the statement:

- President Johnson's military advisers told him that bombing North Vietnam would quickly convince the North Vietnamese to stop their support for the Vietcong. Then the US military in South Vietnam would be able to assist the ARVN to win the war against the Vietcong.

For example, to argue against the statement, one of:

- The resolution was about defending South Vietnam and did not mention attacks on North Vietnam.
- The purpose of the resolution was to protect the USA from open opposition from North Vietnam.

## 20. The mass bombing campaign

For example, any two reasons for the mass bombing campaign from:

- To disrupt the transport of equipment and reinforcements along the Ho Chi Minh Trail.
- To damage the industries that were making the equipment sent to South Vietnam down the Ho Chi Minh Trail.
- To convince North Vietnam to stop supporting the Vietcong.

For example, any two examples about effectiveness from:

- Mass bombing was not able to effectively stop the production of supplies because these were being made mainly in China and not in North Vietnamese factories.
- Mass bombing was not very effective at disrupting the Ho Chi Minh Trail because it went through neutral countries for most of its route, which the USA could not bomb.
- Mass bombing was not very effective at disrupting transport routes because Vietnamese people constantly repaired the damage, meaning that transport routes were quickly opened again.

## 21. Search and destroy

For example, any three from:

- Burning down villages as a punishment for sheltering Vietcong made South Vietnamese locals hate the Americans and increased support for the Vietcong.
- The main aim of search and destroy was to kill Vietcong. Success was measured in body count – the number of Vietcong killed. However, search and destroy missions did not then hold onto the area that had been cleared. As a result, the Vietcong moved straight back in once US troops had left, so US troops were constantly fighting – and dying – in the same areas. This felt like a failure and made it difficult to explain to the US public how progress was being made in the war.
- The Vietcong could usually retreat from any fight with US troops whenever they needed to, into neighbouring neutral countries: Cambodia, Laos and North Vietnam. Vietnam is long and narrow so the borders were never very far away.
- The Vietcong could blend with the local population, wearing the same style of clothes, which made it very difficult to work out whether a village was a Vietcong base or not. Even if hidden weapons or extra supplies were found in a village, it was difficult to know which villagers were Vietcong or were supporting the Vietcong.

## 22. My Lai

For example, any two from:

- Search and destroy caused resentment and hatred against the USA from South Vietnamese civilians. Even when it did not kill civilians, like at My Lai, the missions often burned down homes. And then terrible incidents like My Lai were reported from village to village. All this increased support for the Vietcong.
- Search and destroy tactics were measured in body count. US troops found it difficult to tell who was Vietcong and who wasn't. There was a temptation to count all bodies as Vietcong. The more bodies, the more successful the mission. The problem this created was shown by My Lai, where soldiers shot as many as 500 innocent people and then counted them all as Vietcong.
- Search and destroy missions sent soldiers out from fortified bases to search for Vietcong, engage them and destroy them. This was extremely stressful as the US troops knew an ambush might happen at any time. They often came under fire from Vietcong without seeing their attackers. This happened with Charlie Company. It suggests that it was not a good way to keep US troops motivated.

## 23. The Tet Offensive

For example:

a) The Tet Offensive was a victory for the USA because they – and the ARVN – killed so many Vietcong and NVA soldiers: around 37 000 killed or wounded, about 20% of all the Vietcong and NVA troops in South Vietnam.

b) The Tet Offensive was a defeat for the USA because US public support for the war was badly damaged by the shock of it, which made it much harder for the US government to justify sending thousands more men to defend South Vietnam.

## 24. Demands for peace

1   a) October 1969: huge anti-war demonstrations forced President Nixon to delay bombing campaigns.

   b) Two million: the number of people involved in anti-war demonstrations across the USA in October 1969.

   c) $20 billion: the yearly cost of the war in Vietnam for the USA in 1967, used by Martin Luther King as an argument against the war.

   d) 18–26: the age of men conscripted to go to fight for the USA in Vietnam through the draft system. The draft was a focus of protests against the war.

   e) December 1964: a protest in Washington DC against the war.

   f) 25 000: the number of people involved in the December 1964 demonstration.

2   The contrast between 25 000 people in 1964 and two million in 1969 is a good indication of the growing unpopularity of the war in the USA.

# The ending of conflict in Vietnam

## 25. Vietnamisation

For example, for ways in which Nixon's approach reduced conflict, any one from:
- Withdrawing US troops meant fewer US troops were involved in conflict.
- Vietnamisation also meant US troops often actively tried to avoid conflict.
- Nixon also supported peace talks between South Vietnam and North Vietnam, although these were unproductive.

For example, for ways in which Nixon's approach increased conflict, any one from:
- Bombing of North Vietnam increased in order to pressure the North into accepting peace terms.
- Conflict spread into Cambodia because of secret bombing campaigns on the Ho Chi Minh Trail in March 1969.
- Vietnamisation meant the North Vietnamese saw they were forcing the USA out of the war. This made them even more determined to keep fighting until the war was won.

## 26. The war widens

1  For example, any two from:
- To weaken the Vietcong and the NVA so that Vietnamisation had a better chance of working.
- To put pressure on North Vietnam to agree to a peace treaty that kept South Vietnam free from communist control.
- To prevent the North Vietnamese helping the communist Khmer Rouge gain power in Cambodia and Laos.

2  For example, any two from:
- Public support for Nixon's approach to the war fell in the USA because widening the war increased US involvement rather than reducing it.
- The communist group in Cambodia actually got stronger as a result of US attacks because local people did not like being attacked and North Vietnam increased support.
- In 1971, Congress banned US troops from being used in Cambodia or Laos again.

## 27. Kent State University

For example, any two from:
- Tensions increased between those who opposed the war and those who supported it: those who supported it often justified the shooting of the students – 58% of Americans surveyed blamed the students; those who opposed it were often horrified that Americans were now shooting Americans.
- Tensions increased between student protestors and the government, because many students believed the government would kill more students to stop the protests.
- Tensions increased between those who supported Nixon's approach to the war in Vietnam and those who thought it was not working after the invasions of Laos and Cambodia.

## 28. Media and public opinion

For example, in support of the statement, any two from:
- If the media had not uncovered stories like the massacre at My Lai, then the US military would have kept them covered up. So, any people who felt negatively about the war because of My Lai only did so because of the media.
- People in the USA saw television coverage of the Tet Offensive almost as it happened. Reporters and photographers who followed soldiers on missions saw the reality of the war. All these stories and images influenced how Americans felt about the war.
- When the media reported events such as the invasion of Cambodia, which Nixon announced on 30 April 1970, demonstrations and protests followed.

For example, against the statement, any two from:
- The biggest influence on public opinion was the number of US troops killed in Vietnam. These numbers were released by the US military. They were reported by the media, but people didn't need media interpretation to find them depressing. The more young Americans that were killed, the more people wanted the war to end.
- The majority of Americans continued to support the war, despite negative media coverage. Media coverage of student protests also made many Americans even more strongly supportive of the war, for example the 'hard hats' who attacked students protesting against the Kent State shootings.
- The media was also used to encourage public support for the war. For example, Nixon's 3 November speech to the 'silent majority' used the media: it was on television. The media also reported the enormous amount of support the president received, and the positive polling data in which his personal approval ratings as president increased from 55% to 77%.

## 29. The Paris Peace Talks

You could choose from a number of different reasons, as long as you explain your choice. For example:

Nixon was the main reason for the breakthrough. He accepted that the North Vietnamese could keep their troops 'in place' in South Vietnam while the USA pulled out, which made the North Vietnamese willing to negotiate. Nixon also forced Thieu into agreeing to terms that he knew were likely to destroy his country. Finally, Nixon supported the secret deals between Kissinger and Le Duc Tho of North Vietnam that led to the Accords. He was determined to get the USA out of the conflict at almost any cost.

## 30. The US withdrawal

- Who? This is a crowd of mainly Vietnamese people (some Westerners were among the crowd), many of whom had worked with the USA in Vietnam.
- What? They are waiting for evacuation by helicopter.
- When? 29 April 1975.
- Why? They are hoping to be evacuated from Vietnam before the North Vietnamese take Saigon.
- Where? The photograph was taken at the US embassy in Saigon.

## 31. Reasons for the US defeat

Your answer to this question will depend on your own opinion about the reasons for the USA's defeat in Vietnam. For example, you might write:

The most important reason why the USA was defeated was that the US army in Vietnam underestimated support for the Vietcong in South Vietnam. The USA assumed that the South Vietnamese people would be happy that the USA had come to defend them from communism and would help them defeat the Vietcong. However, this underestimated how unpopular Diem's government was in South Vietnam because of its corruption.

## 32. Vietnam in 1975

For example, any two from:
- What to do with the South Vietnamese who had fought against the NVA and Vietcong, for example people who had been in the ARVN.
- How to rebuild a country that had been devastated by 30 years of war.
- How to convince peasants to let the state take over farming.

## 33. The price of conflict

Many answers are acceptable as long as you explain why the particular cost has been chosen. You should think about:
- the human cost
- the impact on government
- the economic cost
- the impact on both the USA and Vietnam.

# Answers

## PRACTICE

### 46. Practice

**19** The leaflet is very critical of the North Korean leadership because it implies that Kim Il-Sung and his Party leaders are living well by starving the people of North Korea. This is shown in the contrast between the thin, poorly dressed mother trying to feed her distressed and starving child on the left, and Kim Il-Sung, who is shown as well fed and well-dressed, on the right. The purpose of the source was to encourage North Korean people to help the UN and South Korean army to defeat the North Korean leadership. The US was opposed to communism. Many in the US thought that the US leadership had lost China to communism in 1949 and President Truman was determined not to let communism spread any further – and to 'roll it back' if he could by defeating the North.

### 47. Practice

**20** Source L is an aerial photograph of a strategic hamlet in the 1960s. This is useful because it gives an accurate record of what one strategic hamlet looked like at the time. The photograph clearly shows the defences of the strategic hamlet, which consist of several rows of barricades with ditches between them. This is useful because of its content: the photograph demonstrates that strategic hamlets had strong defences. However, a weakness of this source is that it is selective. We do not know if this is a particularly well-protected example, or if all strategic hamlets had these types of defences.

Source M is an official report by an important US official. Officials really hoped the Strategic Hamlets programme would work, and prevent the Vietcong from being able to get support from villages. This may have meant McNamara was biased in his report, or was only shown examples of strategic hamlets that were successful. Source M does include very useful information about the Strategic Hamlets programme in one area of Vietnam, including that villagers were pleased that the VC were no longer able to tax them. It is useful to know that living in strategic hamlets had prevented these villages from being attacked by the Vietcong. However, another weakness of Source M is that it assumes the South Vietnamese people wanted to be protected from the Vietcong, when many of them were disgusted by the Diem regime and did not want to support it.

### 49. Practice

**21** The Gulf of Tonkin incident in August 1964 was when a US warship, the *USS Maddox*, reported that it was under attack by North Vietnamese torpedo boats. Previously, US presidents Kennedy and Johnson had been very keen to keep US troops out of Vietnam. President Johnson's military advisers, however, believed that bombing North Vietnam would quickly stop the North supporting the Vietcong in the South, which would end the war quickly.

As a result, four days after the incident, the US Congress passed the Gulf of Tonkin Resolution, which gave the President the power to use whatever military force he thought necessary in defending South Vietnam from the North. He was no longer limited by a reluctant Congress.

Johnson used the Gulf of Tonkin Resolution to approve Operation Rolling Thunder, which was a campaign of bombing North Vietnam from the air. The bombing resulted in many civilian, as well as military, casualties. This increased international tension because so many people around the world protested against it.

Also in 1964, General Westmoreland told Johnson that he needed many more US troops in order to defeat the Vietcong. Johnson used the Resolution to send more troops. By the end of 1965, there were 200 000 US troops in Vietnam. Westmoreland also escalated the way US troops were used. Instead of defending settlements, they now went out on search and destroy missions. The aim was to wear down the Vietcong. All of these changes increased conflict in North and South Vietnam and only happened as a result of the Resolution: I think this was therefore the most significant event in causing the increase in conflict and tension.

### 51. Practice

**22** Many factors were important in causing the Korean War, and the division of Korea in 1945 was certainly one of the most important. In my opinion, however, the main reason for it becoming an international war was that civil tensions in Korea became part of the Cold War.

The reason why Korea was divided in 1945 was because the USSR had defeated the Japanese in the northern half of Korea and the USA had defeated the Japanese in the south. Two rival governments were set up, led by Kim Il-Sung in the North and Syngman Rhee in the South. Kim Il-Sung was a communist and the USSR's choice of leader, while Syngman Rhee had strong ties to the USA and was a capitalist. Tensions between the two governments increased because of their different ideologies: Kim wanted Korea to be united and communist and Rhee wanted Korea to be united and capitalist. If the North and South governments had not been so influenced by the USSR and USA, war might have been avoided, because really both sides wanted a united Korea that was free from foreign control. It was the developing Cold War between the USA and USSR that intensified the tension between North and South.

Tensions between the two sides turned into war when North Korea invaded South Korea in June 1950. This decision by Kim Il-Sung was definitely a main reason for the war. But, again, the Cold War was very important, too. Kim had been asking Stalin to support an invasion of the South since 1949, but Stalin had said no because he was worried about the USA's response. If Soviet troops ended up fighting against US troops, the USA might use nuclear weapons against the USSR. But, by June 1950, the situation was better for Stalin: US troops had left South Korea, China had become communist and would support North Korea and, very importantly, the USSR had developed its own nuclear weapons. Stalin was also convinced that the USA would not join a war to protect South Korea. That is why Stalin supported the invasion. Without these changes in the Cold War, which made the USSR stronger, the North would have been much less likely to invade the South. This is another reason why the Cold War was the main reason for the Korean War.

The reason the Korean War became a major international conflict rather than just a civil war was that the superpowers became heavily involved. The USA led the UN campaign in Korea. The USA was determined to combat the spread of communism because of the Domino Theory – the idea that, if communism was not contained, one country after another would become communist. The Truman administration in the USA felt that it had lost China to communism. And, without the US-led UN campaign, it is very likely that the North Korean invasion would have succeeded in 1950. By the time the USA sent troops, the North had control of almost all of South Korea. So, if the USA had not acted to stop the invasion, the conflict would have been much shorter and not developed into the Korean War. It would not have involved 16 other UN countries or brought China into it in October 1950.

In conclusion, I do not agree that the division of Korea was the main reason for the Korean War. Instead, I believe the Cold War was the main reason for the Korean War. Although the division was the cause of conflict between North and South Korea, underneath that was the determination of both sides in the Cold War to prevent the other side from influencing other countries into becoming communist or capitalist. Without the Cold War, the USA would not have defended South Korea, and there would have been no advance into North Korea that then brought China into the war. This all shows that the Cold War caused the Korean War.

# Notes

# Notes

# Notes

Published by Pearson Education Limited, 80 Strand, London, WC2R 0RL.

www.pearsonschoolsandfecolleges.co.uk

Text and illustrations © Pearson Education Ltd 2018
Editorial by Just Content Ltd., Braintree, Essex
Typeset by PDQ Digital Media Solutions Ltd.
Cover illustration by Eoin Coveney

The right of Rob Bircher to be identified as author of this work has been asserted by him in accordance with the
Copyright, Designs and Patents Act 1988.

First published 2018

21 20 19 18
10 9 8 7 6 5 4 3 2 1

**British Library Cataloguing in Publication Data**
A catalogue record for this book is available from the British Library

ISBN 978 1 292 24297 2

Printed in Slovakia by Neografia

**Acknowledgements**
Content written by Sally Clifford, Brian Dowse, Victoria Payne and Kirsty Taylor is included.

The author and publisher would like to thank the following individuals and organisations for permission to reproduce
photographs:

(Key: t-top; b-bottom; c-centre; l-left; r-right)

**Alamy Stock Photo:** Everett Collection Historical 2, 8, 17; Archive PL 4cr; Photo 12 5c; Chronicle 9cl;  Granger
Historical Picture Archive 9br; Art Directors & Trip 31; Everett Collection Inc 44, 45; B Christopher 33;
**Shutterstock:** Universal History Archive 4cl; Universal History Archive/Universal Images Group 37; Granger 15;
**Getty Images**: Wilbur E. Garrett/National Geographic 14; MPI 19; Universal Images Group 22; nik wheeler/Corbis
30; Halstead 32; **The Estate of Karl Hubenthal (1963)**: 36.

Pearson acknowledges use of the following extracts:
**p25: Random House:** *The Vietnam War: An Intimate History,* Burns, Ken & Ward, Geoffrey (2017), p421; **p28: CBS:**
Cronkite, Walter, broadcast 27 February 1968; **p37: Linder, Professor Douglas:** *Famous Trials, The My Lai Massacre
and Courts-Martial: An Account* based on the testimony of Lt William Calley, University of Missouri, Kansas City
(© 1995).

**Note from the publisher**
Pearson has robust editorial processes, including answer and fact checks, to ensure the accuracy of the content in this
publication, and every effort is made to ensure this publication is free of errors. We are, however, only human, and
occasionally errors do occur. Pearson is not liable for any misunderstandings that arise as a result of errors in this
publication, but it is our priority to ensure that the content is accurate. If you spot an error, please do contact us at
resourcescorrections@pearson.com so we can make sure it is corrected.